New Directions for
Higher Education

Martin Kramer
EDITOR-IN-CHIEF

Leadership Amid Controversy

Presidential Perspectives

Judith Block McLaughlin

EDITOR

Number 128 • Winter 2004
Jossey-Bass
San Francisco

LEADERSHIP AMID CONTROVERSY: PRESIDENTIAL PERSPECTIVES
Judith Block McLaughlin (ed.)
New Directions for Higher Education, no. 128
Martin Kramer, Editor-in-Chief

Microfilm copies of issues and articles are available in 16mm and 35mm, as well as microfiche in 105mm, through University Microfilms Inc., 300 North Zeeb Road, Ann Arbor, Michigan 48106-1346.

NEW DIRECTIONS FOR HIGHER EDUCATION (ISSN 0271-0560, electronic ISSN 1536-0741) is part of The Jossey-Bass Higher and Adult Education Series and is published quarterly by Wiley Subscription Services, Inc., a Wiley Company, at Jossey-Bass, 989 Market Street, San Francisco, California 94103-1741. Periodicals Postage Paid at San Francisco, California, and at additional mailing offices. POSTMASTER: Send address changes to New Directions for Higher Education, Jossey-Bass, 989 Market Street, San Francisco, California 94103-1741.

New Directions for Higher Education is indexed in Current Index to Journals in Education (ERIC); Higher Education Abstracts.

SUBSCRIPTIONS cost $80 for individuals and $170 for institutions, agencies, and libraries. See ordering information page at end of book.

EDITORIAL CORRESPONDENCE should be sent to the Editor-in-Chief, Martin Kramer, 2807 Shasta Road, Berkeley, California 94708-2011.

Cover photograph © Digital Vision

www.josseybass.com

CONTENTS

EDITOR'S NOTES

The public envisions college or university presidents as well-paid executives in their ceremonial role at graduations, the institution's official cheerleader at ball games, and the smiling greeter at alumni receptions. But presidential duties are not all fun and games, and the visible nature of the presidential position is not always so desirable.

This volume examines the position of presidents during times of great controversy at their institution. Five presidents describe highly charged events on their campuses when constituents disagreed sharply and all were certain that righteousness and virtue were theirs alone. For the president, there was no way to avoid taking a position and no decision that would please, or even appease, all. The presidents describe the episodes on the campuses, explain the decisions they made, and assess their actions retrospectively.

The stories collected here can be read on several levels. First, they provide examples of decision making when interests and principles conflict. In the chapters that follow, presidents must decide who will be the commencement speaker, whether to prevent a student newspaper from printing an advertisement, how to handle a player's charges of discrimination against a coach, whether a controversial food service vendor's contract should be renewed, and what should be the name of a university's athletic team. Complicated management questions in and of themselves, these disagreements also touch on passionately held values of American higher education and American society: freedom of speech, freedom of the press, public safety, democratic processes, race, athletics, and social justice. As the presidents attempt to resolve these controversies, they face both practical and ethical dilemmas—what administrative actions to take and what values to endorse. Their accounts provide readers the opportunity to assess which presidents' actions they support and which they disagree with and to consider what other choices might have been possible. Indeed, one of the chapter authors, Paul G. Risser, in Chapter Six provides two differing assessments of his decision making as the new president of Miami University: his thoughts two years after the controversy had subsided and a further evaluation seven years and a second presidency later.

Second, these cases offer a glimpse into the personal ambivalence of a college and university president at times of great ambiguity, when the "right" thing to do is not self-evident and any decision reached will incur disappointment, anger, and enmity. Although some crises unify people, ideological disputes inevitably pit people against one another, and dissension continues even after a final decision is reached. The usual presidential strategies of negotiation and compromise can be seen as suspect, even illegitimate or immoral. In these stories, readers can see the dilemmas and feel the pressures as the presidents encounter them.

Third, these scenarios provide an opportunity to examine the role of the college and university president. As the pinnacle job in higher education administration, the presidency, although highly visible, has far less real power than is often assumed. Many veto groups and powerful forces within and external to the institution severely constrain presidential prerogatives. Kathy Schatzberg, president of Cape Cod Community College, once commented in a board retreat that she was the hood ornament of the car, not the driver. She wanted the trustees to appreciate that, although they often focused on her as president, her successes resulted from the efforts of many others at the institution. Of course, the hood ornament not only draws attention, it is also the part of the car easily bashed in during an accident.

Outline of the Volume

This volume is made up of six chapters. Chapter One describes three dimensions of presidency: leadership, management, and governance. The first two are familiar concepts, often presented as though they are manifest not only in different competencies but also in different people. Although individuals are likely to favor one or another, the job of president requires both leadership and management. Furthermore, a third competency is required in higher education: a facility with governance. The chapter discusses these orientations and their interplay, providing a conceptual framework for analyzing the cases and for considering the complex nature of the presidential role.

In Chapter Two, Jane L. Jervis describes the decisions she faced as the president of Evergreen State College (Olympia, Washington) when students issued an invitation to a man on death row for killing a police officer to be their commencement speaker. Should Jervis honor the long-established institutional processes that had resulted in this selection, or should she veto the decision because the speaker is inappropriate for this ceremonial occasion? Would giving him the platform as commencement speaker signify that the college values free expression of controversial ideas, or would it glorify murder and show insensitivity to murder victims and the police? Finally, because of the outpouring of anger about the issue, would a decision to proceed with the speaker seriously risk the safety of students, families, and guests at graduation?

In Chapter Three, Edward T. Foote II agonizes over a similar dilemma when faced with the decision of whether to stop the student newspaper at the University of Miami (Miami, Florida) from printing an advertisement questioning the existence of the Holocaust. The advertisement was deliberately deceptive, and the area surrounding the University of Miami is home to the largest number of Holocaust survivors outside of Israel. If Foote were to overrule the student editors' decision to publish the ad, would this constitute censorship of the press? On the other hand, if the student newspaper were not blocked from publishing this ad, would the university be responsible for contributing to the dissemination of misinformation? How should the principles of freedom of speech and freedom of the press be assessed, given the great pain this publication would likely cause?

In Chapter Four, Judy Genshaft, president of the University of South Florida (Tampa, Florida) and her former executive assistant, Jack Wheat describe a controversy that received extensive media coverage and required much administrative attention during the first year of Genshaft's presidency. The allegations of racism in the women's athletic program brought together, as the authors express it, "two potentially explosive issues of modern university life, race and athletics." How should Genshaft proceed to determine what had really happened, create a process that would be viewed as legitimate both on and off campus, handle the intense media pressure on the university and on her personally, and at the same time learn her way around the institution and conduct its regular business?

In Chapter Five, Peggy R. Williams, president of Ithaca College (Ithaca, New York) and Michael R. McGreevey, executive assistant to the president, describe how a seemingly routine administrative decision—whether to renew the contract of the college food service provider—became a politically charged issue on the campus when an activist student organization raised questions about the food service provider's connections to the private prison industry. To the students, the decision was not about finances or quality of service; it was an issue of the college's stance on social justice. The students occupied a building and issued an ultimatum to the president to terminate the newly signed contract with the food service provider. For Williams, the process of ending the sit-in and reaching a decision about the contract became as important as the decision itself, demonstrating the value of open inquiry and open and respectful dialogue.

In Chapter Six, Paul G. Risser examines the importance of process in deciding whether to retain or change the name of the athletic teams of Miami University (Oxford, Ohio), the Redskins. Like Genshaft, Risser faced this hotly contested question in the first year of his presidency. While he was still getting acquainted with the institution, Risser faced a situation in which, in his words, "there were strong and deep feelings on both sides, and both sides could not be simultaneously satisfied." Risser outlines the history of the controversy: how the athletic teams' nickname came into being and what changes had been made over time in the university's use of the nickname, and he discusses how his arrival as a new president served as an opening for the issue to reemerge. His chapter is divided into two parts, the first written while he was still at Miami University and the second with the additional perspective and distance of a second presidency.

Purpose of This Volume

The stories included in this volume are vivid portraits of the dilemmas the five presidents faced when forced to negotiate and reconcile strongly held and widely divergent values and opinions. These chapters are not intended to demonstrate the best way to make a decision or the correct decision to be made. Nor are they presented as fully developed cases that draw on the diverse vantage points of the many participants in each situation. Other individuals would likely tell the stories differently, emphasizing other facts or providing alternative interpretations. As the title of this volume indicates, the chapters represent individual and subjective "presidential perspectives," collected here so that readers can peer over the shoulders of the presidents and understand the situations as they encountered them.

Bringing these stories together was more complicated than it may seem, but not for lack of possible case material. Two presidents turned down, outright, my request for them to write about the controversies on their campuses, citing their time and the sensitivity of the topic as reasons. Several presidents who were asked to contribute chapters to the volume agreed to do so but, after thinking it over, decided that writing about the controversy that had roiled their institution risked rekindling it or at least causing individuals to relive the distress the turmoil had engendered. One president wrote a chapter, only to be advised by the institution's attorney when she was ready to submit it that the incident was still too volatile for public airing. These presidents understood that the best interests of their institutions superseded their desire to tell their stories.

Given the difficult nature of the topics discussed in this volume, I am especially grateful to these authors for their contributions. Their careful presentations of the controversies on their campuses required that they devote considerable time, not just to write the cases but also to do the research necessary to recreate the events. Their willingness to reflect on their decisions, to be honest about what they did or did not know, and to be forthright about what they thought has made their chapters vivid and illuminating.

I am also indebted to the *New Directions for Higher Education* Editor-in-Chief Martin Kramer, who approached me about editing a volume for this series. He stimulated my thinking in our conversations and was both supportive and patient from its conception to its conclusion.

Finally, my deep appreciation to my parents, Gertrude and Seymour Block, emeriti faculty members at the University of Florida, for their excellent advice on this volume and all of my writing over the years, and their inspirational professional and personal examples.

Judith Block McLaughlin
Editor

JUDITH BLOCK MCLAUGHLIN is educational chair of the Harvard Seminar for New Presidents and director of the Higher Education Program at the Harvard University Graduate School of Education, where she has been a member of the faculty since 1984.

1

Presidents are expected to articulate vision, devise plans, and facilitate decision making. These different dimensions of the job are sometimes complementary, but they may also compete for the president's attention or suggest contradictory ways of proceeding.

Leadership, Management, and Governance

Judith Block McLaughlin

When a college or university anticipates a presidential vacancy and readies for the search, one of the first tasks of the board of trustees or the search committee is to draft a job description that will serve as a guide for the recruitment, screening, and selection of candidates. Typically, every board or committee member's favorite ideas are included on the long list of presidential duties and desired character traits for the new president, resulting in an impossible and often self-contradictory ideal. But if the description is of little help in evaluating candidates, it is revealing as a statement of the constituents' various images of the presidency.

In this chapter, I group these diverse assumptions about and expectations for presidential performance into three categories, leadership, management, and governance. In his classic formulation, Abraham Zaleznik, an organizational theorist and psychoanalyst, claims that leadership and management are two separate sets of attitudes, behaviors, and orientations found in two different kinds of people with divergent personal histories, temperaments, and psychosocial needs (Zaleznik, 2004). Although college and university presidents may have more in common personally with one of these characterizations than the other, their presidential post requires that they assume both leadership and management roles. Moreover, because in higher education, central authority is suspect and collaboration and collegiality are sacred values, college and university presidents must also operate in a third arena, *governance*. Although it could be argued that what is referred to here as governance is subsumed under the categories of leadership and management, a college and university president's facility with governance is so essential to his or her success in the job that this dimension is fully deserving of its own category.

In their leadership role, college and university presidents are called on to attend to the ideas, ideals, and individuals of their institutions. As managers, presidents serve as their institution's chief executive officer, responsible for, as former Stanford University President Gerhard Casper noted (as quoted in Muller, 2000), "teaching and research, academic clinical care, and a dizzying array of product lines" (p. 276). Finally, with regard to governance, presidents serve at the point of intersection of many diverse constituencies with differing, competing, or colliding priorities, interests, values, and perspectives. They must serve as mediator, translator, negotiator, and facilitator so that the institution is not continually in a state of governance logjam. To characterize these ideas succinctly: leadership answers the question "what," management answers the question "how," and governance answers the question "who." Or, to put it more playfully, leadership is inspiration, management is perspiration, and governance is incorporation (using the definition "to cause to merge or combine together into a united whole" [Webster's, 1998]).

In this chapter, I define these dimensions of leadership, management, and governance; explain their relevance to the college presidency; and provide illustrations of them in presidential language and actions. In doing so, I offer theoretical insights into the stories of campus controversies that follow and provide a framework for understanding the complexities of the presidential role.

Leadership

In a college presidency, leadership is characterized by a focus on the values, purposes, and meaning of the institution, both as an affirmation of its raison d'etre and as a mandate for change. Presidents are expected to connect individuals to the mission of the enterprise, to raise sights, and to encourage hopefulness in the future. Yale University President Bartlett Giamatti explained: "leadership. . . . is an essentially moral act, not—as in most management—an essentially protective act. It is the assertion of a vision, not simply the exercise of a style" (quoted in Weems, 1993, p. 2).

In his presidential inaugural address at Dartmouth College in 1987, James Freedman proposed a new vision for the college and image of the students it should attract. Dartmouth, he said, should seek "those singular students whose greatest pleasure may come not from the camaraderie of classmates, but from the lonely acts of writing poetry or mastering the cello or solving mathematical riddles or translating Catullus. We must make Dartmouth a hospitable environment for students who march to a different drummer—for those creative loners and daring dreamers whose commitment to the intellectual and artistic life is so compelling that they appreciate, as Prospero reminded Shakespeare's audiences, that for certain persons a library is 'dukedom large enough'"(Freedman, 1987, p. 14). This notion of the student who marches to a different drummer became a motto for the new direction in which Freedman wanted the college to move. It served as a mission statement for the admissions office, a rallying point for faculty who wanted the college to be more intellectual in tone, and the object of criticism and derision from alumni who interpreted it, accurately, to signify an intention to move Dartmouth away from the fraternity-dominated college world they had known. Whatever people thought of this idea, Freedman's leadership in articulating it was unmistakable.

Like Freedman, all presidents are expected to produce "vision statements" for their institution. Unlike Freedman's address, however, few of these statements would be judged eloquent or imaginative; most are generic and derivative in their rhetoric, with institutional direction couched in such general terms as to offend no one. "In reality," Richard Chait (1993) notes, "the daily lives of most faculty and many staff members are seldom directly affected by presidential visions" (p. B1). Yet, this truth stops neither presidents from trying to assert vision nor institutional constituents from asking for it, in large measure because the hoped-for vision represents a deep desire to have one's work and workplace acknowledged as worthy. Presidents as leaders respond to this deep need in people to feel connected to something bigger than themselves.

Controversies such as those described in this volume thrust college and university presidents into leadership roles. Presidents serve, as University of South Florida President Judy Genshaft states in Chapter Three, as "the standard bearers for the academic and ethical principles of the institution" (p. 35).

If the values are lofty ideals about which all agree, the responsibility of standard bearer is relatively easy to assume. In times of disagreement, however, when presidents are forced to assert some values over others, the position is far more hazardous. When University of Miami President Edward T. Foote II decided not to prevent the student newspaper from printing an advertisement questioning the existence of the Holocaust, he explained his choice in terms of the values of freedom of the press and freedom of speech. Some trustees, faculty, and students argued that he should have based his decision instead on the values of truth and compassion. In reflecting back on his decision (in a conversation in a Harvard Graduate School of Education class, Nov. 2001), Foote recalled a statement made about the Supreme Court: that it is at its best not when deciding between right and wrong but between right and right. He understood that his decision required him to select between two strongly compelling positions and that he would deeply disappoint some people with whichever choice he made.

As leaders, presidents operate in the symbolic realm where images and interpretations are often more salient than what actually occurs in any situation. Unable to discuss publicly the particulars of the discrimination charges against a University of South Florida employee, Genshaft (see Chapter Three) found that allegations had traveled far and wide and that she needed to respond not only to the actual situation but to the larger prevailing assumptions about the campus racial climate, the place of athletics at the university, the alleged cover-up of charges, and other issues and accusations speeding along the rumor highway. Similarly, for Peggy R. Williams, president of Ithaca College, the Young Democratic Socialists' charges against the college's food service provider, Sodexho Marriott Services, became "the truth" to many students long before any facts about Sodexho's political and financial connections were known (Chapter Five). Presidents also discover that they, themselves, become symbols, serving, in the words of David Riesman, as the "living logo" of their institutions (personal communication). As such, their words and actions are carefully noted and extensively interpreted, making it impossible for them to drop the leadership mantle, even when they may want to do so. Although Jane L. Jervis (Chapter Two) made the decision, in consultation with the members of her board of trustees, senior administrative cabinet, and leaders of the faculty, to proceed with a controversial commencement speaker, she was the target of much of the hate mail that poured into the college.

Management

Whereas leadership constitutes attention to what events and decisions mean to participants, management is concerned with how to get things done (Zaleznik, 2004). Leaders articulate vision; managers develop strategies and plans. The emphasis of management is on rationality and control, on tactics and results (Zaleznik, 2004). As managers, college and university presidents work to align institutional resources—money, technology, and personnel to solve problems or forge new institutional directions.

No matter what grand ideas they may have, presidents find that their job requires them to react much more often than to initiate. Most items that arrive in a president's "in basket" call for managerial responses, and these daily tasks are the real meat of the job. Robert Birnbaum (1988) notes that presidents "influence through the smaller things they do—their choices as to which letter they will answer and how . . . or naming the members of a campus-wide committee. It is the incremental effects of many actions that together make certain outcomes less likely and other outcomes more likely" (p. 213).

Managerial responses in daily business transactions, then, may over time result in leadership directions. Conversely, management may be, more intentionally, the infrastructure by which leadership ideas are executed. When John Lombardi was asked to reflect on his presidency of the University of Florida, he spoke in management terms: "To know if you're getting better you have to be able to measure things," Lombardi explained (quoted in Sanoff, 2001, p. 38). He described how he implemented his plan for the university:

> The measuring process for driving the university toward a higher level of competitiveness and improvement involved a structure that looked at productivity and quality. . . . On the productivity side we included enrollment, grant contract revenue, private giving, and revenue streams generated by other income. . . . The other half of the conversation related to quality. Each college was required to construct a quality measurement system. . . . As part of the process, there was national benchmarking . . . to guarantee that there was always a reference point that was constant, steady, and better. . . . As a result, when it is time to deliver incentives you have a matrix of data that allows you to have a data-driven conversation. . . . (Sanoff, 2001, p. 40).

Lombardi also instituted new computer systems to allow deans to manage money and students to track their own academic progress. These structural changes carried with them incentives and rewards to encourage cost-saving behaviors. Commented Lombardi: "All of this came about simply by hearing the noise and finding out the systemic problem that the noise is a symptom of" (Sanoff, 2001, p. 68). Lombardi's goal was to achieve greater efficiency and enhanced performance, and he saw management systems as a means toward this end.

In times of controversy, as the stories in this book attest, college and university presidents face complicated management problems as well as leadership issues. How do they obtain the necessary information with which to make their decisions? What is the nature of the problems needing attention, and what actions and strategies will best address these? How should these be implemented? What might be the short-term and long-term consequences of these decisions?

When Evergreen State College President Jervis decided to proceed with Mumia abu Jamal as the college's commencement speaker, she knew that the management plans she made would be essential to support the values this leadership decision represented (see Chapter Two). Put bluntly, if she did not do all that she could to ensure that graduation was safe and orderly, there was a real risk that she could be sacrificing the occasion—or in the worst case scenario, the safety of people—to the ideals she had articulated. In addition to explaining why she supported the students' choice and articulating the underlying values it signified, Jervis had to manage the event carefully, overseeing the execution of public safety provisions, communications plan, and media relations. Managing the media was a major concern for all five presidents who share their experiences in this volume because the controversies on their campuses quickly turned into sound bites on television and rich fodder for radio talk shows, further exacerbating the situation. As local disagreements became national debates, the resulting press coverage, letters, and e-mail correspondence required extensive administrative attention. Crisis-management plans became essential considerations, too, as institutions without well-developed protocols, like Ithaca College, created them, and those with plans in place, like Evergreen State College, made alterations to fit the crisis before them.

Governance

On most campuses, presidents have little real executive power. Even the best ideas and plans come into being not as a result of presidential declaration but by presidential persuasion. Governance entails enlisting others effectively; it involves balancing the interests of multiple constituencies and respecting the process of decision making. Presidents who are most skilled in this area know when and how to involve others. They gather input, understand and respect differing perspectives, elicit support, develop partnerships, and create a sense of engagement and ownership. With these efforts, they gain support for their initiatives, or at least ensure that they will not be vetoed. The process of decision making is lengthened, but the likelihood of decisions being seen as legitimate is increased.

Duke University President Nannerl Keohane explains this governance perspective well: "Making things happen boils down to getting other people to do things in order to achieve your end; in energizing other people, harnessing their energies, directing their attention. . . . Making things happen means building coalitions, forming alliances, compromising in order to get further, and working with other people whose purposes converge with yours in order to reach some common goals" (1985, pp. 35–36). According to Keohane, presidents must regard others in the institution "as genuine colleagues in a common enterprise, as co-laborers in the same vineyard, to accomplish common goals" (p. 37).

The attention to governance is evident throughout the cases described in this volume. Although Jervis knew that the final decision about the commencement speaker rested with her, she understood that making this decision alone would violate the nearly sacred norms of consultation at her college. In Chapter Two, she describes how she turned to senior staff, faculty, student, and community leaders for advice on what to do (what leadership decisions to make) and how best to do it (the management planning). As president of Miami University, Paul G. Risser (Chapter Six) established an elaborate process of consultation when faced with the decision about whether to keep or to change the name of the university's athletic teams. Knowing that there were passionate feelings on all sides of the question, Risser held a day-long open forum at which all university constituents could speak, and in a bow to the importance of process and the symbolism of the presidency, he stayed for the entire day to listen to the outpouring of opinions.

Although both leadership and management are important capacities for a president, a facility with governance is the sine qua non. Presidents without vision can languish; presidents with ideas but no skills at implementing them can find others to manage for them. But presidents who do not know how to govern effectively will find their aspirations thwarted and their tenures short-lived. As one board of trustees chairman commented to me about the former president of that institution, "He had all the right ideas, but he stepped on all the wrong toes." The president's tenure lasted barely a year.

New presidents are not alone in their failure to understand the importance of the governance dimension of their position, however. Longer-term presidents not infrequently make the same mistake. Whereas earlier in their tenure they appreciated the need to honor campus governance processes, longer-term presidents grow accustomed to making decisions and begin to shortcut the process, sometimes unwittingly and other times deliberately. Birnbaum (1992) has noted that presidents with longer tenures no longer seek out faculty opinion as they had done when they were beginning office. The early "listening campaigns" in which presidents make a concerted effort to touch all campus bases are things of the past. On campus, presidents spend more time working in their offices and less time walking around and seeing campus constituents. Off campus, the fundraising that takes increasingly large bits of their schedule is especially seductive. Not only are the trappings that accompany these conversations with alumni and donors appealing—lovely settings, good meals, interesting company—many presidents discover that talking about the institution's successes and future possibilities is more enjoyable than responding to the seemingly endless and repetitive petty grievances and mundane matters at the campus. The tangible victory of raising money often trumps the vaguer sense of achievement at the institution. And the attention paid presidents in their ceremonial role can be heady. The result is, sadly, that once-popular presidents, who had received acclaim for their accomplishments in an earlier day, lose their support and wreck their reputations when they forget the critical nature of this concept of governance to their jobs.

In the stories presented in this volume, the presidents were at different points in their presidencies when the controversies developed. Two presidents, Genshaft and Risser, were new to the job; two presidents, Williams and Foote, had been in office for several years; one president, Jervis, was in her last year of office, having just announced that she intended to retire from the presidency at the end of the next academic year. The timing of a controversy in a president's tenure carries with it different issues and problems. The arrival of a major controversy early in a presidency forces the new president to make decisions before knowing important information about the institution—who are the right and wrong people to consult, what are the expected protocols and processes for decision making, and what is the history of the issue and what might be its connection to previous disputes and agendas. New presidents may step on landmines without being aware they are there or use up nonrenewable political chits early in their presidential career. Their actions with regard to this controversy constitute the powerful first impressions that campus constituents and external audiences have of them as president. For midterm presidents, these controversies serve as a reminder that unforeseen events can upend a presidency at any time. Unlike the new presidents whose actions are the first evidence the campus has of their presidency, the responses of these presidents to the controversy are joined to the opinions others already have of them, giving new fuel to their opponents and running the risk of incurring additional critics. The old quip about the presidency applies here: in a college presidency, friends come and go and enemies accumulate. For a president at the end of a long tenure, a controversy of this kind threatens to be the lasting memory of the presidency, displacing all the good work that has preceded this final incident.

Complementary, Competing, or Contradictory?

The three dimensions of the college presidency—leadership, management, and governance—represent different ways of assessing and addressing situations that can be compatible and complementary. Although each offers a somewhat different analysis and course of action, together they may compose a more thoughtful approach than any one of these perspectives would provide alone. All the presidents who wrote for this volume took on leadership, management, and governance roles in the stories they relate: they articulated the larger values that underlay their decisions, implemented the plans to carry them out, and involved others in these activities. The ordering of these roles may not be as predictable as this suggests, however. The leader's larger vision for the institution may emerge from, rather than precede, the management functions or be a by-product of time spent with governance.

Sometimes, though, a choice must be made between these alternate positions because the course of action that one dimension of the job dictates is counter to that which another dimension recommends. In these instances, which should prevail? Risser questions, in his most recent reassessment of how he handled the Redskins controversy (see Chapter Six), whether he paid too much attention to governance considerations at the expense of management prerogatives. But what might have been the consequences of his having proceeded differently? Likely he would have expedited the decision-making process, but in doing so he might have encountered other difficulties if campus constituents had become angered that their opinions were not heard.

The choices and trade-offs are complicated for presidents because expectations for their performance are often inconsistent or contradictory. As chief executive officers, presidents are expected to manage their institutions effectively, but as they attempt to make pragmatic and strategic decisions, they are criticized for failing to understand or appreciate the heart of the enterprise. Although attention to governance is necessary to win support, presidents who emphasize participation are accused of not doing enough or not moving fast enough and are said to be unable to make decisions. Presidents are called on to exercise leadership, but their initiatives are resisted and considered threats to institutional community. Standing tall in the academy, they discover, is more likely to make them a target than a hero.

Because there is no agreed-on job description, there can be no simple formula for balancing the different roles of the presidency. As the stories in this volume suggest, presidents look to their own values and listen carefully to their environments for clues about how to proceed. Their institution's culture and circumstances make some choices more viable than others, and external political realities provide additional guidelines.

In the end, they do the best they can, proceeding with some combination of good judgment and skill, counsel, and luck to make the decisions they believe best serve their institution.

References

Birnbaum, R. P. *How Colleges Work: The Cybernetics of Academic Organization and Leadership.* San Francisco: Jossey-Bass, 1988.

Birnbaum, R. P. "Will You Love Me in December as You Do in May? Why Experienced College Presidents Lose Faculty Support." *Journal of Higher Education,* 1992, *6,* 1–25.

Chait, R. "Colleges Should Not Be Blinded by Vision." *Chronicle of Higher Education,* Sept. 22, 1993, p. B1.

Freedman, J. O. *Speaking at the Outset: Four Addresses by President James Freedman at Dartmouth in 1987.* Hanover, N.H.: Dartmouth College, 1987.

Keohane, N. O. "Collaboration and Leadership: Are They in Conflict?" *College Board Review,* 1985, *135*(spring), 5–6, 35–37.

Muller, H. "I Have at Least Nine Jobs." *Fortune,* Oct. 16, 2000, *142*(9), 275–288.

Sanoff, A. P., "Speaking on the Record." *University Business,* Apr. 2001, *4*(3), 37–40, 47, 68.

Webster's Revised Unabridged Dictionary. Springfield, Mass.: Merriam-Webster, 1998.

Weems, L. H. "Leadership as a Moral Act." *Presidential Papers,* 1993, *9*(2), 1–6.

Zaleznik, A. "Managers and Leaders: Are They Different?" *Harvard Business Review,* originally published Mar.-Apr. 1992; republished as *Harvard Business Review Classic,* January 1, 2004, pp. 1–9.

JUDITH BLOCK MCLAUGHLIN is educational chair of the Harvard Seminar for New Presidents and director of the Higher Education Program at the Harvard University Graduate School of Education, where she has been a member of the faculty since 1984.

2

National controversy erupted when students at a public university invited a man who was on death row for killing a police officer to speak at their graduation ceremony.

Many Faces of Risk: Free Speech Versus Public Safety

Jane L. Jervis

On June 11, 1999, The Evergreen State College (Olympia, Washington) prepared to celebrate commencement. Some seven thousand people crowded the square under bright sunshine. Over eleven hundred graduates, most in green caps and gowns but many as usual in exotic costumes, milled about greeting friends and shepherding families. Political placards blossomed; graduates and guests wore ribbons and armbands proclaiming their allegiance to one cause or another. From ever-more-distant parking spots, latecomers arrived tired and sweaty. On several tables around the periphery, bottled water was for sale. Staff members serving special duty as ushers and coordinators tried to guide people to seats or to various staging areas. It might have been an ordinary graduation day at Evergreen.

But my eyes focused on the extraordinary. Thick bundles of cables connected multiple satellite trucks with a special media platform overlooking the stage. Representatives from about three dozen national and regional news organizations swarmed through the crowd. Armed campus police officers watched from rooftops, while a large group of off-duty police formed an honor guard for Maureen Faulkner. Faulkner held a photograph of her husband Danny, a police officer killed on duty in Philadelphia in 1981. Mumia abu Jamal,[1] on death row for eighteen years for the murder of Daniel Faulkner, was to be one of our graduation speakers.

It was clear from the symbolism of protest that you either supported the police, law and order, and America or you supported Mumia abu Jamal. Supporters of Mumia abu Jamal wore yellow armbands, distributed informational leaflets featuring a caged bird on a yellow background, and carried yellow banners showing a caged bird. Police supporters wore blue ribbons and armbands and distributed literature explicating Mumia abu Jamal's guilt. Because this was Evergreen, a few people (including some Evergreen police officers) wore both blue and yellow, and many faculty wore signs that said, "Learning Across Differences." A full-sized replica of an electric chair was borne aloft: I saw my name around the neck of the dummy strapped into it.

I went through the motions: brunch with distinguished guests, last-minute adjustments to the script, robing and photo ops with the platform party, guiding them across the square to where we would lead off the academic procession, and the procession itself. As I stood on the platform watching students march, amble, or dance (or all three) to their seats through a double column of faculty, honoring them, I wondered if we were doing the right thing. Did the principles of free speech, democratic process, and educational autonomy really outweigh the undeniable risks to public safety and institutional reputation? Were we about to see American democracy at its finest, or was this the opening act of a tragedy?

In the last few days, I had been feeling in my palms the fur coat of a woman whose son died on my watch at another campus nearly twenty years earlier—not my fault but surely my responsibility—to my deep and lasting grief. He had been found unconscious by the campus police and was put to bed by them, presumed drunk, instead of being taken to the hospital. I was his dean. How would I feel if we had a tragedy at this graduation, knowing that I may have had the power to avert it?

This is a story of the many faces of risk.

Background

The Evergreen State College is a public university in Olympia, Washington, the state capital. Opened in 1971, Evergreen is known for its innovative curriculum featuring interdisciplinary, team-taught academic programs with a strong emphasis on putting theory into practice. Evergreen is seen as politically liberal (even radical by its detractors), and Evergreen students and faculty are frequently engaged in political activism. It is an institution that takes its principles seriously, debates them fiercely, and tries to institutionalize them in practice.

Evergreen's commencement ceremonies are joyful, sometimes raucous, events featuring an array of speakers—faculty, undergraduate and graduate students, sometimes staff and alumni, and an outside speaker chosen by graduating students. Outside speakers have frequently been controversial, either in themselves or in what they say. Shortly after my arrival at Evergreen, the speaker was Leonard Pelletier, who sent a speech from federal prison where he is being held for the killing of Federal Bureau of Investigation agents. There was no public controversy over Pelletier's speech although, like Mumia abu Jamal, he was at the center of an international grass-roots political movement. Pelletier spoke to our graduates about the transforming power of education, a message that gained power from his own circumstances.

In 1999 the senior class selected Mumia abu Jamal as a graduation speaker. A number of students had been studying the criminal justice system and were deeply concerned about issues of race, social justice, and the death penalty. The selection was controversial even on campus, but the selection process was open and student-controlled. The governor, a centrist Democrat, had also been invited and had agreed to speak, knowing that Mumia abu Jamal would be on the program via a brief audiotape.

In early May, a reporter publicly challenged the governor on "sharing the stage with a cop killer." The ensuing controversy made national headlines, and the governor withdrew from the program. A national campaign of threat and intimidation was unleashed against Evergreen and against me, waged through the Internet, e-mail, talk radio, the U.S. mail, and the U.S. Congress. In about six weeks, I received over seven thousand pieces of mail. Some of the letters were moving and troubled, concerned about violence in our society, but most were themselves violent, racist, and full of hate.

I had been president of Evergreen since August 1992. In August 1998, I had announced to the board of trustees that I would retire in June 2000, and in early April 1999, I had publicly announced my retirement. The board had already constituted a search committee. During the uproar over graduation, there would be many external demands that I be fired, but the institution and the board stood with me.

Mumia abu Jamal

Mumia abu Jamal is no ordinary "cop killer." He was convicted for the murder of Philadelphia police officer Daniel Faulkner on December 9, 1981. He is African American and had been a Black Panther and later a journalist who exposed and campaigned against police brutality in Philadelphia. During the years that he has been on death row and through multiple judicial appeals, Mumia abu Jamal has continued to write and speak out on issues of criminal justice, centering on the nexus among race, poverty, criminal prosecution, and the death penalty. He has become an icon of the international debate on these topics.

He and his supporters maintain that he is innocent. Many who are not certain of his innocence nevertheless maintain that he did not have a fair trial. (On December 18, 2001, a federal judge again upheld his conviction but threw out the death penalty, ruling that the jury had been improperly instructed and that a new hearing within six months was needed to determine the penalty; failing that, his sentence would be converted to life imprisonment without parole.)

Evergreen did not take a position on whether Mumia abu Jamal was innocent or guilty; some students and faculty clearly believed in his innocence while others equally clearly believed he should be executed. The public campaign against Evergreen asserted that our having him as a speaker meant that we believed he was innocent, that we did not accept judgment by a jury, that we were glorifying a murderer, that we supported the killing of police officers, and that we were indifferent to the suffering of crime victims and the widows and orphans of officers killed in the line of duty.

Our position was that the courts had not taken away Mumia abu Jamal's right to speak, that our students had chosen him as a speaker to address one of the significant issues of our day, and that a college campus (and Evergreen in particular) had to stand for free discussion of controversial ideas if it stood for anything.

We were taken by surprise by the scope and vehemence of the opposition. There had been no public reaction to Pelletier's speech just a few years before despite the similarity of their circumstances. But we were naïve about the ways in which the two cases differed. We were not aware of how hot this issue was in the mid-Atlantic states, nor of how powerful the police fraternal organizations were and how skilled at mobilizing the media (notably the Internet and conservative talk radio).

Public Response

By mid-April we were inundated by phone, mail, and e-mail. For the next two months, the work of the president's office was nearly brought to a halt. We received some twenty-seven hundred letters from people who identified themselves as working in law enforcement. Of these letters, about 97 percent were form letters, many of which arrived in bundles. Letters from New Jersey, Maryland, and New York accounted for 68 percent of the total. Only 3 percent of these letters came from Washington State, and fewer than half of the Washington letters were form letters. I personally received more than three thousand e-mails, and as graduation approached, we were getting over two hundred phone calls a day.

We had no way of analyzing whether there was significant overlap among the types of communication. Many callers would not leave their names; many e-mail correspondents had coded "monikers," and many signatures were illegible. Finally, we just counted and made rough categories. We judged that we had heard from substantially more than seven thousand people. We responded to nearly all individual correspondence, including e-mails (although not to the form letters), and tried to respond with information and open exploration of issues and principles.

I received a few dozen letters or e-mails from thoughtful correspondents who were concerned about the level of violence in this country and whether our actions would help or harm children. This was the year of Columbine, where the students who killed others and then themselves saw themselves as disenfranchised outcasts. Rightly or wrongly, the lesson we drew from Columbine was that our society needed urgently to bring those voices into the public conversation, not to further suppress them. Many correspondents were troubled about student autonomy, wondering whether our schools had not gone too far in abdicating power to students, who were after all children. We ought, they argued, to tell them what to do, not allow them to decide for themselves. (The average age of our graduates in 1999 was over 33.)

But by far most of the responses showed little thought or insight into the issues involved. The form letters were certainly of this kind, and most of the e-mails had the feel of form letters or at least contained certain standard phrases and expressions that clearly indicated a common source. Discussion on national or regional talk radio, for example, would prompt a spate of indignant calls, e-mails, and letters all using the same language. I believe that the nastiness of the correspondence was enhanced by the medium of e-mail, which gives users the illusion of anonymity. And I believe that the volume and uniformity of the correspondence was clearly an artifact of the Internet and of conservative talk radio, both of which mobilize huge audiences almost instantly. Some examples:

> YOU are a DISGRACE to all that is good and moral in this country and it is because of people such as yourself that this country is on the continuing downward spiral into hell that it is. Stop making this COP KILLER into an icon, stop glorifying this COP KILLER! [this passage verbatim in scores of e-mails]
>
> Do me a favor. . . . each time you pass a POLICE OFFICER, give him or her the middle finger to tell them how you feel about police in general. By having a COP Killer give that speech, that's the way I believe you feel.
>
> YOU ARE FUCKING PEA-BRAINED IDIOTS—your pseudo-intellectualism based on racial and gender anxiety is fucking garbage.
>
> What kind of sick human being are you to let such a lower than human being like this Jamal character, give a speach [sic] at your school.

We were able to attribute much of the mail to Officer Down (a Web site focusing on officers killed on or off duty), COPS (Concerns of Police Survivors), the Law Enforcement Alliance of America, and other police fraternal organizations and to the Daniel Faulkner Web site.

After twenty years in academic administration, I thought I was incapable of being shocked by any form of human behavior, but I was shocked and shaken by the level of viciousness and hatred displayed by many of my correspondents, most disturbingly by members of the law enforcement community. Many hoped that I or my loved ones would be brutally attacked and that, when I called for help, Mumia abu Jamal would come instead of a police officer and kill me. Some called for the immediate, brutal, and long-overdue killing of Mumia abu Jamal and referred to him in violently racist terms:

> Just saw on 20/20 that you guys actually had that guilty nigger speak at your commencement. . . . I hope that guilty nigger is electrocuted soon!!!!!!!!

> Hey, Is this the idiotic school who likes negros? Especially ones that kill people. Did ya assholes ever think about the poor woman much less the man who gave his life, protecting good people from nigger animals like what the shit his name is. The dumb ass who ok'd this should lay down with the nigger when they finally put the scuz bag where it belongs.

In the final days as we agonized about whether to go forward, one of my personal struggles was to try to separate out my own motives. Was I acting on the basis of clearly-thought-out rational principles? Or was my back up, and was I simply reacting against this worst kind of bullying?

I received only a handful of statements of support until after the ceremony, when a number of people said they had been supportive all along.

Legislative and Executive Response

As a public institution located in the state capital, the youngest and smallest of Washington's four-year institutions and the most unconventional, Evergreen has always been particularly subject to legislative scrutiny. Since its founding there have been periodic calls to abolish Evergreen, often in reaction to student activism. Indeed, one of my principal occupations as Evergreen's president was making the case for our unconventional but highly effective educational program to skeptical or even hostile legislators and members of the press. I was assisted by the fact that over the years, Evergreen graduates had come to occupy key positions in government, in business, and even in the governor's office.

Despite episodes of inflamed rhetoric over the years, Evergreen had been well treated by the legislature and regularly drew at least its fair share in the state budget process. Among many legislators, in fact, Evergreen had the reputation of being an institution that advocated for public policies on principle rather than out of institutional self-interest.

Fortunately, 1999 had a short legislative session, and when the graduation controversy exploded, the legislature was not in session and our biennial budget was not actively being debated. Nevertheless, we were very concerned about communicating with legislators and conveying to them a more balanced account than was being presented by the press. We were about as successful as we expected to be. Our traditional supporters understood what we were trying to do and supported it. Some legislators were willing to consider and understand but disagreed with what we did, often on the grounds that graduation was an inappropriate venue for political activism. And some, of course, saw this simply as one more outrageous act by an outrageous institution:

> Be assured that this unacceptable (honor) of allowing a cop killer to speak will result in grave political consequences. . . . I must inform you that my future support in regards to your college will certainly depend on your treatment of this critical matter. [state representative]

If the leadership at Evergreen wishes to be the center of controversy in the name of perverse objectivity, so be it. But know that your dishonorable actions leave a stain upon the community that will not soon be forgotten. [state senator]

On a day when your graduates ought to be hearing words of encouragement, hopefulness and optimism for their country and their future, you have instead elected to denigrate a taxpayer-supported institution by providing a public forum for the convicted murderer of a police officer. [state representative]

Evergreen's controversy even reached the U.S. Congress. In a press release dated June 8, 1999, Representative Tom DeLay, the majority whip, said:

I am shocked that Evergreen State College would invite convicted cop killer Mumia Abu-Jamal to speak at its commencement ceremony. . . . In today's culture, with tragic mass murders occurring in schools across the nation, it is socially irresponsible and morally abhorrent of Evergreen State President, Dr. Jane Jervis, to allow this killer to speak to her students. If Dr. Jervis continues to insist that Abu-Jamal speak at the graduation ceremony, I will join Mrs. Faulkner and the students by holding a moment of silence on the floor of the House of Representatives on June 11th to protest this egregious act.

The governor of Washington, although his office had played a role in the genesis of this controversy, did not at any time reproach me or Evergreen or suggest in any way that we should excise Mumia abu Jamal from the ceremony. In the ensuing weeks, he never criticized Evergreen's decision, nor did he allow members of his staff to do so. In fact, when an Evergreen student aide in his office said that he would not attend graduation in protest of Mumia abu Jamal's speech and in support of the governor, the governor sent him to graduation.

Media Response

During the weeks leading up to graduation and on the day itself, there was what I can only describe as a media frenzy centered on Evergreen. On June 10, the day before graduation, the *New York Times* ran a long and well-balanced article in their "National Report." That was a striking exception. Most newspaper and television accounts focused on conflict or the possibility of conflict: the governor against the college, legislators against the college, police against the college, the widow against the college's president, and law-abiding citizens against criminals and radicals. Editorial positions were universally against us.

For weeks we were the focus of conservative talk radio from as far away as Florida. I am not particularly good at rapid-fire aggressive verbal jousting, so I declined to appear on these programs, but a couple of members of my senior staff took part on several occasions. They enjoyed the sparring, but it is doubtful that they changed any hearts or minds.

Our greatest frustration was that we felt we were unable to get a serious presentation of the complex educational issues that were at stake in this controversy. I wrote editorials, visited editorial boards, gave interviews, and wrote letters to the editor, which amounted to "spitting in the wind." I had a thoughtful interview with a correspondent of National Public Radio for over an hour and hoped that we might finally receive a public hearing, but even they distilled it into nothing more than a sound bite.

On the morning of graduation, I came to an improvised television studio in the college library at 4:30 A.M. to appear on CBS's *The Early Show.* Faulkner was in the CBS studio in Seattle. We were interviewed separately but appeared together on a split screen. She spoke movingly about her murdered young husband. I spoke about the principles of free speech and student determination.

The news coverage of our graduation by the local newspaper was balanced despite opposition from their editorial board, although in the weeks before, they covered only the most sensational aspects of the controversy. Reporters from the national press left campus muttering, "There's no story here." Coverage was finished, except for a few lingering letters to the editor.

How Speakers Were Chosen

I will describe in some detail how speakers were chosen for graduation because it shows how we gradually were drawn into what became a crisis.

Planning for graduation at Evergreen was in the hands of a committee composed of members of the graduating classes (graduate and undergraduate) and student affairs staff members, under the direction of the dean of Enrollment Services, who had overall responsibility for graduation. The process, which had been in place for many years, was loosely structured and left a good deal of discretion to the committee. They determined the music, the class slogan, design of the program, the number and selection of speakers, design of the graduation T-shirt, and so forth. For student speakers, they held auditions. For outside speakers, sometimes they simply solicited nominations and created a ranked list from the nominations, which they forwarded to the president's office. Sometimes they held an election or referendum to choose from among the nominees. The president then invited speakers, working down the list. There was a strong tradition and expectation that the president would not interpose any personal judgment but would simply work from the committee's list.

For some time, I had been unhappy about the process of selecting speakers. The committee's list usually began with celebrities whom we had no possibility of attracting with our austere budget. We asked the same people year after year and, because we had to wait for a reply before moving on to the next person on the list, we frequently ended up issuing invitations embarrassingly late. Because of a personnel change, we postponed revising the selection process for just one more year.

In 1999 nominating the outside speaker drew scant response from students. The governor received by far the most nominations (about thirty from a graduating cohort of about eleven hundred). Mumia abu Jamal had a handful. A number of other candidates received one or two nominations each. The committee deliberated whether to put the names up for a runoff ballot and decided not to. They weighed the work and expense of setting up an election against the likely participation rate and concluded that they had enough information to proceed. Their decision was within precedent.

Acting on the committee's recommendation, in early January I sent a formal invitation to the governor. Over the course of the next month, there was some confusion about whether he would be able to speak. Believing that the governor had declined, most of the students present at the next committee meeting supported inviting Mumia abu Jamal. Bypassing the president's office, some students issued a direct invitation to him to participate by sending an audiotape, and he accepted. A brief notice appeared in the local paper mentioning that Mumia abu Jamal was under consideration and that the governor had not yet made a decision. We then learned that the governor was, in fact, available.

What a mess! The graduation committee deliberated long and hard and received input from a significant number of students. Student support for having Mumia abu Jamal as the speaker was burgeoning. The Tacoma program, with more than a hundred adult students (most of whom were persons of color), sent a statement that their students unanimously supported Mumia abu Jamal's participation. The committee concluded that the governor should be the keynote speaker as originally planned and that Mumia abu Jamal should not be considered a keynote speaker. Rather, they said, the audiotape from Mumia abu Jamal should be included among the speeches by the student, faculty, staff, and alumni representatives. This seemed a reasonable resolution to an unfortunate situation, devised by a legitimately constituted student committee, and I concurred, as did the governor.

On April 8, an article in the student newspaper implied that there would be two keynote speakers sharing the podium. In mid-April a reporter publicly asked the governor why he was sharing a stage with a convicted cop killer. It made the national news, and the governor's office was inundated with protests. The governor invited me to his office and told me that he was going to have to withdraw. He relied on the state patrol for the safety of himself and his family. He had no choice about this decision, he said.

In response to the loss of the keynote speaker, some students proposed making Mumia abu Jamal the keynote speaker. By this time, it was clear to me that a major external controversy was developing and that issues of public safety and institutional well-being were involved, and I chose this moment to intervene in support of the structure of the graduation committee's decision. I instructed the vice president for student affairs to identify a keynote speaker from within the Evergreen community. Faculty member Stephanie Coontz, a skilled public speaker and a popular teacher, was an inspired choice. By April 27, I announced to the campus the resolution of the commencement speaker controversy. Coontz was to be the keynote speaker, and Mumia abu Jamal's tape was to be included among the "other" speakers later in the program.

I expected an internal outcry against my intervention. There was none. I think that by this time it was evident that the controversy was larger than anyone had expected and that many, including some on the graduation committee itself, were privately relieved.

In early June, Maureen Faulkner, widow of the slain police officer, publicly asked for equal time at graduation to rebut Mumia abu Jamal's comments (which she assumed would profess his innocence) and to present her side. She published her text in a full-page paid announcement in the local paper. We refused, prompting a wave of angry correspondence. Why did we support free speech only from the radical left? We refused because we were not sponsoring a debate over Mumia abu Jamal's innocence; because her appearance would have added fuel to the sensationalist aspects of the media coverage and raised the risks to public safety; and because the debate was already taking place in every corner of the campus and across the country, but it was only Faulkner's "side" that was being covered by the media.

One aspect of the controversy that raged on and off campus was that the decision to invite Mumia abu Jamal was made by so few people that it could not be said to represent student choice. I was urged to overturn the decision because the participation rate was so low. I would like to dwell on this question in some detail because it was one of the fundamental principles I was to return to again and again in the coming weeks.

First, focusing on the initial number of "votes" or nominations was beside the point. The graduation committee used those nominations as guidance, but as the process unfolded, they made a decision based on their best judgment and on their reading of campus sentiment, as revealed to them through petitions, letters, e-mails, and personal contacts. I wish that they had conducted a referendum. They did not, and that decision was within their discretion. I did not agree to include Mumia abu Jamal's remarks because a handful of students had nominated him. I agreed because a duly constituted student committee, working within guidelines that had been long established, struggled with the controversy and determined that this was the way they wanted their graduation structured.

My conversation with the governor sharpened my realization that my decisions needed to be made first and foremost from the perspective of the leader of an academic institution, a teacher. The governor made a political decision, as was perhaps appropriate for a political leader. But whereas political considerations always play a role in the actions of the president of a publicly funded university, the primary mission of the university is educational, and our most powerful teaching tool is example. We teach by what we do.

What would we be teaching? That student apathy is justified because student-made decisions can be set aside by the president? That duly constituted committees are empowered to make decisions only so long as the president likes what they come up with? That protest trumps process?

I returned again and again to Evergreen's fundamental educational principles—that we learn best by doing and that we learn most in difficult conversations across deep differences. In her keynote speech, Coontz said, "What really makes Evergreen special is that we don't just take differences in stride. We seek them out, to test our own beliefs, no matter how much we expect to disagree with the other side. We work to listen seriously to each other. And then we try to bridge our differences without papering them over. There is no skill you will need more in the kind of world into which you are about to graduate."

Many people argued that graduation should be a celebration, that learning belonged in the classroom, and that we were dishonoring our graduates and their families by bringing conflict to this occasion. Parts of me agreed. I would not have sought out this controversy for our graduation. But I felt strongly that fleeing from it by overruling legitimate student decisions would have dishonored Evergreen and taught lessons in political expediency and avoidance of conflict that should shame an academic institution. I believe that Evergreen's graduation offered a profound learning experience and that most of the lessons were good. I believe that we were also very lucky.

There were rich ironies here. I conceived of my decision as educational, not political; yet, the lessons that were at stake were political ones. The lesson I was concerned with was fundamental democratic political process. It seemed even more ironic that a public university, whose mission ought to highlight preparation of an informed and engaged citizenry, should come under fire for attempting to do just that.

Postscript: During the closing weeks of the academic year, I imposed an interim process for choosing the next year's speaker, pending a participatory redesign to be engaged in by the community in the next academic year. (Such discussions typically take a full year at Evergreen.) Student participation was much higher than in 1999, and the outside speaker was Matt Groening, creator of *The Simpsons* and a graduate of the college. What a contrast between the serious passions of commencement 1999 and the lightheartedness of 2000!

Public Safety

As we considered the risks involved in proceeding, the physical safety of students, employees, and guests of the college weighed heavily. There are always some risks involved in hosting a large number of people in confined spaces. We were particularly concerned in this case because of the viciousness of the public discourse. Recent instances of unbalanced people opening fire in crowded places because of real or imagined grievances were fresh in our minds.

Customarily, Evergreen employed off-duty police officers from surrounding jurisdictions to supplement our own campus police. For this event, we were unable to hire a single additional person. The boycott was complete. We were unable to get additional on-duty officers assigned to us. If there was an emergency, we were told, officers would be dispatched to help, but until something bad happened, they would not be available.

Evergreen's Office of Police Services was a relatively new organization. One of the highly controversial decisions earlier in my presidency was to arm our public safety officers and to make them fully commissioned police officers. We had a relatively new chief, and most of our officers were recently hired or recently trained (or both); I had commissioned all of them myself. This was a difficult assignment for them. They were under great pressure from off-campus colleagues. I heard early rumors of a possible sick-out.

Our police chief was a full participant in our planning discussions. He made a number of recommendations about improving the safety of the campus, adjusting the width of aisles and blocking access to the roofs, for example, and he assured us that his officers could be counted on. All shifts would be on duty. He was confident that, in the event of violence, the off-duty officers who were there to protest the event would behave constructively and professionally. I hoped he was right.

But it was in this area of safety that we struggled hardest with the balance between supporting our educational principles and preserving the peace. Were the principles of sufficient heft to balance out real risk to life and limb? Baldly put, what if students died on June 11?

Our final decision was that, in the absence of any specific threat, we would go ahead with the ceremony, taking all possible precautions. If we received any threats or any credible information that violence was planned or beginning, we would immediately cancel the ceremony and evacuate the campus. This would, of course, carry its own risks: of panic, of counter-protests, and of the loss of the day for our graduates and their families.

How Decisions Were Made

In much of this narrative, I have deliberately used the first person plural, and I would like now to address the issue of internal governance and decision making at Evergreen. Evergreen is an intensely collaborative institution. It has an educational commitment to collaborative learning and to interdisciplinarity. Governance is shared to an extraordinary degree.

It was established practice that I met weekly with my senior staff: the vice presidents and the directors of college relations, legislative liaison, and budget; the secretary to the board; and my executive associate. These were freewheeling discussions of policy, direction, planning, and principle. Most decisions were made by consensus. Expansive discussions and brainstorming were the rule, and all of us, including myself, could count on having our dumb ideas thoroughly exposed, debated, and evaluated. Any one of us struggling with a decision could thrash it out with this group of smart, engaged, and respectful colleagues. This gave us as a group exceptional creativity and security. It was certainly not the most efficient way to govern, but it ensured a remarkable breadth of perspective and confidence in our decisions.

It was this group that struggled with the issues relating to graduation, that agonized, strategized, and advised. There were disagreement and doubt, fear and courage, and passionate argument about principles. There was never any doubt that the final decision of whether to go ahead or not was mine, but I would never have made that decision without their input and support.

Evergreen has a governing board, seven trustees appointed to staggered six-year terms, and one student trustee appointed to a one-year term, all by the state's governor. The board met monthly, although it was experimenting with meeting every other month. The board has a very clear delegation of authority to the president, with precise exceptions to that delegation. If I were ever in doubt about where my authority met the board's, I would take it to them. "I think this is my decision," I would say, "unless you tell me you want to make it." Or the reverse.

My cardinal rule for board relations was never to allow my trustees to be taken by surprise. I told them everything, especially the potentially bad things. We always talked about the principles that informed decisions.

As a result, there was an unusual level of trust between me and my board, and the trust was unusually well informed. Of course, I kept the board fully informed as this situation developed. They agreed it was my decision. I asked them individually to tell me candidly if at any point they got cold feet about the way we were moving. They never did. Every member of the board was on stage at graduation, and they played an important role in interpreting Evergreen's actions to the wider community. I was enormously proud of the role they played.

Graduation Day Itself

I was mistress of ceremonies at graduation, and I hoped that by strongly modeling ceremony, decorum, and civility, I would be doing what I could to set a tone that the audience and participants would be caught up in. I introduced a number of deviations to the standard script. I started, using flight-attendant tone and gestures, by describing the exits from the square, pointing out which exits had stairways, and asking people to identify the nearest exit. This drew a laugh, and I felt the crowd relax.

I then gave a detailed exposition of the symbolism of the day, the meaning of commencement, the traditions arising from medieval times, and the entry of our graduates into the community of scholars. I talked about the role of protest and dissent and articulated the particular conflict of the day:

> Absolutely fundamental to Evergreen's educational philosophy is the belief that it is in the clash and argument and resolution of different perspectives that creativity and tough-minded critical thinking emerge. To listen thoughtfully, respectfully, seriously, critically to a point of view is not necessarily to agree or endorse or glorify the speaker. If we listen only to those we know we will agree with, we may as well speak only to ourselves, and we can guarantee that we will never be disturbed, stretched, or changed.
>
> Maureen Faulkner is present at our ceremony today. She is the widow of Daniel Faulkner, a police officer who was killed on duty in 1981. Later in the program we will be hearing a recorded statement from Mumia abu Jamal, who was convicted of killing officer Faulkner. The national reaction to including abu Jamal's remarks challenges us all to reach within ourselves—to find that place where we can be respectful of the pain and outrage this has caused Maureen Faulkner and police officers and their families—and in the same moment to affirm the importance of listening to someone whose perspective and experiences are very different from theirs.
>
> As we recognize today your achievements at Evergreen, confronting differences and learning to regain balance through respectful dialogue are among the most important achievements that we will celebrate.

When I introduced Mumia abu Jamal's tape, I said the following:

> Some people have said that they wish to leave during this part of the program, or to stand and turn their backs. I would ask that you respectfully facilitate those expressions of conviction, and that you allow people to leave and return quietly. I would also ask that you make it possible for those who wish to listen to do so.

Before the tape began to play, about a dozen graduating students walked out, and another two dozen or so stood and turned their backs to the stage. A few dozen members of the audience, including Faulkner and her police honor guard, left as well. A few Mumia abu Jamal supporters stood and faced the stage. The tape was of low fidelity and difficult to understand, but the audience was absolutely silent. The knot that had been growing in my chest (and stomach and neck and . . .) for the past two months began to relax. When the tape was over, there was applause and cheering, and when the students who had left returned to their seats, their classmates stood and cheered them. I wept with pride.

The next day, the local paper featured a front-page graduation story. The headline: "Grads Take Turmoil in Stride." A six-by-nine color photograph shows a sea of green mortarboards. A uniformed police officer, with mortarboard, stands at parade rest with his back to the stage. Directly facing him, one row back, two students stand holding a yellow banner with a caged bird on it. All three of the faces are in repose. All three are listening intently. The photograph says it all.

And the speech itself? It was published in full by the local paper, and we made transcripts available after the ceremony. Citing the Declaration of Independence, Mumia abu Jamal spoke in support of struggle against a government that does not consult or represent the governed. He identified his heroes in the struggle (most of whom were unknown to the audience), and he called on the graduates to work for freedom. He did not mention his imprisonment, nor his guilt or innocence. Astonishingly and ironically, I never heard anyone refer to the content of his speech, that day or afterward. It was the fact of his speech that was controversial and significant.

Mornings After

The moment graduation ended, the external firestorm was over. Evergreen disappeared from the news and from talk radio as if nothing had ever happened. I continued to receive correspondence, now mostly from people who attended graduation reflecting on what they had learned, and most were positive.

We got a number of calls and letters from alumni who knew about what had happened only from the media. Their questions were so persistent that in July I sent a long letter to all alumni and parents describing graduation and attempting to explain what the issues were. This itself prompted a few new angry responses.

That fall, the American Civil Liberties Union of Washington, no stranger to controversy in support of principle, gave me its Civil Libertarian Award, "for courageous defense of freedom of expression and students' rights." This was the first sign that anyone outside of Evergreen understood what we had been trying to do.

The following spring, we learned that students at Antioch, in Yellow Springs, Ohio, decided to follow Evergreen by inviting Mumia abu Jamal to speak at their graduation. I offered to share our experiences and advice with the president of Antioch. Antioch's situation was similar to ours, with two exceptions. First, because Antioch is a private institution, the controversy did not raise the same fury about public support and did not raise the threat of legislative action. Second, there were ugly confrontations between students and police on the day of graduation.

On balance, did graduation 1999 help or hurt Evergreen? Anecdotally, we know that we gained a few enrollments and lost a few, gained a few financial supporters and lost a few, and made some people angry at us and some proud of us. We gave new ammunition to our traditional detractors and to our traditional supporters. By the standard indicators of institutional health, there would seem to have been no lasting effects. The educational effect in the minds and hearts of our students is impossible to measure.

Reflections from Retirement

More than two years later and thousands of miles from Olympia, I have found the time and distance to reflect on the events of that day. Did we do the right thing? Would I do it differently if I had the chance? Are there larger lessons to be learned, particularly in the changed world after September 11, 2001?

I would not have chosen this form of controversy for Evergreen. I would not have chosen to risk the festivity of graduation for a political cause. Most of our students struggled hard to complete their degrees. Many were the first in their families to attend, let alone graduate from college. Graduation was a really big deal for them. They came to graduation with their parents, grandparents, spouses, partners, and children. They were surely entitled to purely celebrate themselves.

I would not have chosen this way to promote public discussion of the issues of race, criminal justice, and the death penalty. A large-scale symposium with distinguished speakers from many perspectives would be the canonical academic route to take. In the current political climate, even this might well have prompted criticism of Evergreen and demands that the legislature rein us in and raised the issue of free speech and the appropriate role of public universities. Attendance would likely have been modest, and I doubt that passions would have been engaged, but at least there would have been the opportunity to reflect analytically on any opposition to the discussion.

On the other hand, graduation 1999 provided an extraordinary learning experience—not only on that day and in that place. The debate raged on campus, at home, over the Internet, in the press, among our students and their families, in classrooms at Evergreen (and perhaps elsewhere), in committee meetings, over coffee or beer or meals, on campus paths and city buses, and in carpools. Students (and others) really cared about this, were engaged deeply in it, and believed that it mattered. What educator would not want this? What I most regretted was that we did not have the opportunity for critical reflection as a community because the community dispersed for the summer. However, knowing Evergreen, I am confident that this controversy received detailed scrutiny in classrooms both in the spring of 1999 and subsequently.

What was deeply uncomfortable for me, as president, and for the academic establishment was that we were not really in control of either the learning context or the outcomes, and in this business, we like being in control. We were holding onto this tiger by the tail and hoping we could prevent it from savaging anyone but reluctant to destroy it. It was high-risk, outside-the-box, heart-in-the-throat institutional behavior.

I would not have chosen it. But like most crises, this one crept up on us. By the time we recognized it as a crisis, we were already in it, trying to make the best decisions we could in a situation that was far from ideal. In retrospect, once we were in it, I think we did the right thing. Not in every detail, not at every moment or in every interaction, but on the whole, I believe that Evergreen acted as a public university in a free society should.

Although I was not conscious of it in the heat of the controversy, in retrospect I believe that I had been deeply influenced by Ronald Heifetz's *Leadership Without Easy Answers* (1994). Heifetz describes a style of leadership that confronts people with clashes of their own deeply held but contradictory beliefs (democracy and segregation, for example). If the leader succeeds in keeping the contradiction at the center of the agenda while preventing chaos, then the stakeholders will eventually resolve the contradiction themselves and probably in the direction of their "higher" natures.

Universities have not always acquitted themselves well as venues for free discussion. I came of age during the McCarthy era, daughter of immigrants who were political refugees from Italian fascism. I remember passionate and horrified discussions around the dinner table as many universities, public and private, submitted to public and political pressure to "discipline" faculty members.

I was made aware of a more local example. As reported by Gary Huxford (1969), in the winter of 1961–1962, the secretary of the American Communist Party and perennial presidential candidate Gus Hall was forbidden to speak at any public college in Washington State; he did speak at the Oregon College of Education in Monmouth (now Western Oregon State University). The public furor was different in detail from that at Evergreen but similar in tenor, with one striking difference: "The press was remarkably uniform in support of the college's position" (p. 377).

In the aftermath of September 11, the American Council of Trustees and Alumni, a conservative watchdog group, in their report, "Defending Civilization" (Martin and Neal, 2002), names faculty members who made remarks in public or in the classroom that the council construed as critical of national policy and therefore unpatriotic and unacceptable on college campuses. Still more recent was an attempt by the University of South Florida and Florida's governor to fire a Palestinian professor who made statements hostile to Israel. In an editorial on this case, the *New York Times* (Jan. 27, 2002) said, "The First Amendment protects not only those whose ideas Americans like but, more important, those whose ideas they abhor. American universities are the envy of the world partly because they encourage robust debate. . . . Free speech and academic freedom must be blind to politics" (p.12).

The forces of political correctness that many believed had run amok on college campuses in the 1960s and 1970s now seem increasingly to be coming from the right and to be calling on the powers of the state in their support.

September 11, the ensuing war on terrorism, and the public and journalistic response have also made me reflect on those kissing cousins, justice and revenge. In the name of justice, we are prepared to suspend due process and civil liberties to "get" those we know are guilty, and we do not much care if individually they really are guilty. It is all the more painful for us because those who are immediately guilty of the attacks on New York and Washington, D. C., are already dead. We do not want justice—we want revenge. And because we know, down deep, that this is not really what we stand for, we must build up and sustain our rage to justify acting vengefully, perhaps because we cannot face our fear. What was really destroyed on September 11 was our belief in America's inviolability.

This insight helped me to understand the viciousness of the attacks on Evergreen, on Mumia abu Jamal, and on me. Law enforcement officers and their families know that they daily put their lives on the line. This sense of threat, of embattlement, contributes to the tight bonding of the police fraternity. When a member of that fraternity is killed in the line of duty, all that fear, that daily dread, is mobilized and takes the more acceptable form of a passionate cry for "justice." The venom of their attacks, their indifference to the possibility that Mumia abu Jamal may not have received a fair trial, and the elaborate national organization they have built to sustain their rage all persuade me that their real (and deeply human) desire is vengeance.

But one of the things that makes us a civilized society is that we have developed systems of law and criminal justice in which we hope that dispassionate and even-handed judgment substitutes for the unbridled application of individual or group vengeance, however natural, human, and understandable the wish for vengeance may be. I was chilled to see the naked face of vengeance looking out from within the very structure of law enforcement.

September 11 and its aftermath, including the deaths from anthrax and the panic that ensued, also caused me to think again about risk and safety. I am reminded of an Evergreen employee who, when we were struggling to clean up a "sick" building, refused to enter the building unless I could guarantee that she would never get cancer. We have a national obsession with safety. We believe that we are entitled to be perfectly safe, and if any harm comes to us, we look for someone else who must be at fault and whom we can sue for damages or who will compensate us for the harm. In planning for graduation, I, too, wanted assurance that everyone would be safe. My rational self knew that was impossible, completely independent of Mumia abu Jamal. People have been trampled to death at rock concerts and soccer matches. Crazed people have opened fire on innocent crowds and on school children. September 11 taught us that going to work or taking a plane or opening a letter might kill us. There is no perfect safety. But I knew I would be held responsible (and I would hold myself responsible) if people got hurt at Evergreen's 1999 graduation.

Time and distance have allowed me to think about the difference between hot and cold issues. Emotions are hot. Principles are cold. "He shot my husband!" is very hot. "We are defending freedom of expression!" is icy. "Fireman Joe died rushing into that building!" is hot. "We should analyze our foreign policy in the Middle East!" is cool. The media increasingly focus on hot issues. Evergreen never had a chance in the public arena to present its cool, logical, and principled arguments in the face of hot emotional ones. We were speaking different languages. We came across as heartless, unfeeling, and perhaps the worst insult of all, academic.

I do not believe that the mainstream media were engaged in any kind of a conspiracy against Evergreen. But I do fault them for their focus on conflict and potential disaster, for their breathless chasing of fire engines, and for pandering to sensationalism. I fault them for failing to identify and comment on the concerted effort by a powerful and well-financed array of police fraternal organizations and conservative groups that focused their resources and the power of the media against a small and already controversial public college.

Finally, I am forced to acknowledge that the heat generated by this event and, yes, even the risk created an extraordinary educational opportunity for everyone present. The uproar itself demonstrated how much what we were doing mattered. By riding out the risk, as a community we opened ourselves to deep learning in ways that are rare in the classroom. There is perhaps no venue other than a campus in which this could have taken place. Colleges and universities must find the courage and the support to engage meaningfully (and perhaps experientially) in the critical issues of the day, even if doing so entails risk. To avoid the risk may court the greatest danger of all: that we will fall into mindlessness and apathy and fail our students.

Note

1. In this chapter, I have used Mumia abu Jamal's name in full throughout. There is no uniformity in the press. The name in Arabic means "Mumia, the father of Jamal." To refer to him as Mumia seems to many people to be disrespectful, as if I am using his first name. He refers to himself by his full name.

References

Heifetz, R. A. *Leadership Without Easy Answers.* Cambridge, Mass.: Belknap Press, 1994.
Huxford, G. "An Incident at Monmouth." *Journal of Higher Education,* 1969, *40*(5), 369–380.
Martin, J. L., and Neal, A. D. *Defending Civilization: How Our Universities Are Failing America and What Can Be Done About It.* Washington, D.C.: American Council of Trustees and Alumni, 2002.
"Protecting Speech on Campus" [editorial]. *New York Times,* Jan. 27, 2002, section 4, p. 12.

JANE L. JERVIS was president of Evergreen State College, Olympia, Washington, from 1992 to 2000. She currently is a consultant in higher education and management.

3

When the student newspaper editors plan to publish an ad questioning the existence of the Holocaust, the issue "burn[s] throughout the community." Should the president prevent the ad's publication? What principles and values should enter into his decision?

Freedom and Controversy on Campus: The Holocaust Questioned

Edward T. Foote II

The worst controversy in my twenty years as president of the University of Miami began innocently enough. In the spring of 1994, I dropped by a student gathering on my way home. An editor of the *Miami Hurricane,* our student newspaper, approached me with several questions. What did I think of censoring, he asked. Did the university have the power to censor the student newspaper? Would it ever do so? Had that ever happened? What was my position on freedom of the press? I began to get the idea that these were more than philosophical inquiries. After some general discussion with what had now grown to many students, including other student editors, my young interrogator explained the reason for his intense interest. The newspaper had received a request to run an advertisement that raised questions about the veracity of the Holocaust, and our editors were agonizing over whether to run it.

Thus began for me and my colleagues a period of reflection, debate, and emotional turmoil that none of us will ever forget. The advertisement turned out to be the same one that had disrupted many college campuses across the country in recent months. A Bradley R. Smith, on behalf of the "Committee for Open Debate on the Holocaust," claimed there was a lack of evidence to support belief in the Holocaust, specifically challenging the validity of information in the U.S. Holocaust Memorial Museum. The advertisement did not deny outright that the Holocaust had happened. Rather, it raised a series of questions about the museum's "technique," calling it a "mixture of sinister suggestion and dishonest omission." The advertisement was a pseudo-historical critique with an obvious bias but cloaked in seemingly legitimate inquiry.

NEW DIRECTIONS FOR HIGHER EDUCATION, no. 128, Winter 2004 © Wiley Periodicals, Inc.

A reader ignorant of the Holocaust may have been led to wonder what was true and what was not. Smith had tried to discredit history, raise questions, and generally confuse readers with unsubstantiated skepticism about overwhelming evidence that Hitler's Germany systematically murdered millions of innocent people. The approach was bound to enrage many people. It was apparent that the students themselves were deeply divided about whether to publish the advertisement. Shortly after I first learned of the problem, our vice president for student affairs and other university officers met with the student editors, who told them that after much debate and editorial soul searching, they had decided to publish the ad.

Meanwhile, of the dozens of other colleges and universities that had grappled with the same advertisement, some had published it, some had not. None, according to reports from many colleagues around the country, had found the decision easy. Many student newspapers operated completely independently. Students made the decisions, one way or the other, and published without prior review before their universities knew about it.

This was normally the case at the University of Miami. There was no prior administrative review of news and editorials. The newspaper editors and editors of other student publications were responsible to a university board of students, faculty members, and administrators, which functioned somewhat like a publisher but did not normally review material before publication. In the case of the Holocaust advertisement, however, the students had brought their dilemma to this board seeking advice and guidance. Payment of money for the advertisement was involved, bringing the university's accounting system into play and alerting administrators to the problem.

All of this happened during the week of April 3, 1994. Because of the controversial nature of the advertisement, the news spread rapidly. Many people learned about it during the same period that I did. By the end of the week, April 8, the student editors had made their final decision. They had approved the decision to run the ad, made originally by the business manager, who had received Smith's letter, advertisement, and check.

Controversy Becomes Public

In retrospect, it was inevitable that this emerging drama would leak to the mainstream media. On Saturday, April 9, the *Miami Herald* ran an article headlined, "UM Paper Accepts Ad Questioning Holocaust" (Gonzalez and Muhs, 1994). My telephone started ringing at dawn. The controversy had entered the public arena, beginning with Miami, Florida, a community comprising many different ethnic groups, including a large Jewish population. More Holocaust survivors lived in Miami than in any other American city. I remember when I moved there in 1981 being struck by the palpable sense of this tragic history that would suddenly push into a conversation as someone would quietly say he or she had lost four or eight relatives or would pull back a shirtsleeve to display a tattooed identification number from the death camps.

As I read the *Herald* article early in the morning, I could begin to understand the dimensions of what would follow. The local antidefamation league official, as quoted, said that if the ad appears, "It will advance a cruel, direct, and painful attack on the Jewish community." The article reported that the vice president for student affairs would be meeting with me over the weekend to decide what the university should do. In fact, I met with many people in the next two days. My calendar reflected the usual busy university president's weekend: a women's track and field meet, a law school visiting committee meeting, a fundraising gala aboard a cruise ship in the port of Miami, a meeting of community leaders to resist—once again—an effort to legalize casino gambling, and a meeting with leaders of the board of trustees. At each of these gatherings, I sought advice about the Holocaust ad. And at each, and elsewhere, I received additional advice, unsought. Following the leak to the media, the issue was now burning throughout the community.

Seeking Advice

Among the most important of these meetings was with my own closest advisors, the "agenda committee," which comprised the senior university officers, the provost, vice presidents, and others who helped me lead the university. Most of us had worked together for many years. All had strong opinions. Some favored allowing the ad to run. Many favored stopping it. Several mentioned their own family tragedies in the Holocaust. Some became more emotional than I had ever seen them in many years of close collaboration.

My other key meetings, some specially scheduled, some by chance, included trustees. The university was and is blessed by an excellent board of trustees, large in the tradition of many private research universities, and highly committed to the institution. The university occupies a special place in the Miami community. Not only is it the only private research university in the entire state, it is also the second largest private employer in Miami-Dade County. Trustees take their fiduciary responsibilities seriously. They, like other groups with which I consulted, were divided. The Jewish trustees especially warned against an explosive reaction in the community if the advertisement ran.

Making the Decision

As the weekend of April 9, 1994, came to a close and the deadline for decisions arrived, I met one last time with a handful of my closest colleagues and advisors. Together we went through the arguments, pro and con, once again. By then, I had had several days of advice from many people. It was time to decide. As is so often the case with leaders, there comes a time when the advice becomes repetitive; the issues are as clear as they are likely to get, and further delay will not help. I believe in following instincts—and in taking long walks to help the thinking process. I took one last walk, talked one last time with my wife, and decided to let the advertisement run.

It appeared on Tuesday, April 12, 1994, in a sense anticlimactically because the essence of the advertisement and the controversy had been public for several days. But now the student newspaper had accepted the money ($288) to publish an advertisement written by a known Holocaust revisionist. (The editors of the student newspaper contributed the money to the Holocaust museum.) My reasons for allowing the advertisement to run are found in my statement to the student newspaper, the *Miami Herald,* and elsewhere in the media the same day the advertisement appeared.

Because my statement is the best expression of my struggle regarding the decision and my reasons for making it, I include it in full here:

> Two fundamental interests are contending today at the University of Miami: our need to understand the unspeakable tragedy of the Holocaust—and prevent another one; and the search for truth in a free society. Student editors of *The Miami Hurricane* have decided to publish an advertisement entitled, "A Revisionist Challenge to the U.S. Holocaust Memorial Museum." The advertisement asserts that the museum "displays no convincing proof whatever of the homicidal gassing chambers."
>
> In no chapter of history have human beings surpassed the monstrous evil of the Holocaust. War, killing, and injustice have been with us always, but never has any government implemented a policy of religious and ethnic extermination on so grand and sickening a scale. Having twice visited in Israel the deeply moving Holocaust Memorial, Yad Vashem, and toured the death camp at Dachau, I will always be horrified that people—many people—could have been capable of such bestiality. I hope I understand the anguish of the persecuted and especially the surviving relatives of the dead, whose anger and pain I have witnessed so poignantly these last few days.
>
> Many students and others have appealed to me as the president of the University to stop the advertisement from appearing. After many hours of consultation with students, colleagues, and friends from the community, and not a little soul-searching, I have decided not to overrule the editors' decisions. Appalled by the Holocaust, why would I allow in a University publication any challenge to a central, widely documented fact? The answer lies deep in the essence of that second fundamental interest, the search for truth at a University. Universities exist as institutions to help human beings learn, and through learning, to lead the best, most productive and happiest possible lives. At the heart of the enterprise, whether in a classroom or in the creation of a book or poem or scientific experiment, is intellectual freedom.
>
> Students and faculty members are free at universities to question, challenge and wonder, to agree or disagree, to form their own opinions, to defend

their own beliefs, and to shape their own values. The founding principle of universities is that through the free exchange of information and ideas the most truth, and from it the highest human understanding, [is] are likely to emerge. People in universities are free to be wrong as well as right, to advance and defend outrageous propositions, to change their minds. From the time of Socrates, at least, the beginnings of understanding have been questions.

Probably no students anywhere recently have searched their consciences and values more than our student editors on this issue. Each in his or her way was doubtless as repelled and mystified by the Holocaust as the rest of us, but decided as journalists, nevertheless, to allow someone to challenge the massive evidence of the Holocaust. The editors made their own decision. They made it in freedom. Others would have decided otherwise. Obviously, people of good will can disagree on such a decision. It is not surprising, given the complexity and emotion of this issue, that some student editors elsewhere (e.g., at Brandeis, Duke, Michigan, and Notre Dame) have accepted this advertisement, while others (e.g., at Berkeley, Columbia, Harvard, and Yale) have rejected it.

Now, the decision is mine. As a student editor, I would not have run the advertisement. As president of the University, however, the standard for my decision must be different. It is not what I would have decided if I were a student editor, but whether the discretion exercised was within reasonable limits that should be allowed student editors. Despite my abhorrence of the Holocaust, I believe the students' decision to be within those limits. The division of student editorial opinion elsewhere on whether or not to run the advertisement makes the point. I concede that the question is close, and that others will disagree with me, but at a University of all places, we should err, if at all, on the side of freedom of thought.

The best antidote for error is not to suppress it but to expose it to the truth. It is important now for our University community to bring forth and reinforce that truth about the horrors of genocide. Those same student editors in this issue of the *Hurricane* have already begun. Ultimately, I do not believe that the two fundamental interests are in conflict. The best human hope for avoiding another Holocaust lies in freedom and knowledge.

Controversy Continues

My view was not universally shared, of course. The other view is best reflected in the statement by Arthur Teitelbaum, Director of the Anti-Defamation League, that appeared opposite mine in many publications. Teitelbaum (1994) wrote,

> If *Hurricane* editors feel that it is important for their readers to know of Bradley Smith's ideas, they could have easily addressed that issue without publishing the advertisement, thereby serving as a billboard for bigotry. Smith and his cohorts target campus newspapers for several reasons. Because they

are often able to manipulate the idealism and naiveté of campus editors into believing that what is *really* an issue of hate on campus is an issue of free expression. And because it's a quick way to inject the poison of anti-Semitism into the bloodstream of the campus, and by generating controversy, the larger community.

The core of the Holocaust deniers' strategy is to create the sense that there are two sides to the existence of the Holocaust, and that through debate the "truth" will come out. The reality is, there is only one side. The Holocaust happened. To debate the historical existence of the Holocaust—or to legitimate such discussion—is not to engage in an intellectually valid exercise, but to participate in a circus of hatred.

For many days, members of the university community talked of little else. The story was now national, having been picked up by the wire services. My colleagues and I did our best to keep lines of communication open, recognizing the real pain the advertisement had caused many, and to seize the opportunity for the maximum education possible about systemic genocide. In addition, in impromptu debates and countless references in classrooms across several campuses, students, assisted by the vice president for student affairs, organized a "campus forum" on the controversy. More than three hundred people attended. I spoke, as did many others. Most opposed the running of the advertisement. The crowd included several Holocaust survivors, whose statements were gripping and poignant.

Meanwhile, the story had become internationalized with the widely publicized threat of a major donor to withdraw his support of the university. Specifically, he threatened to cancel a $2 million pledge, thus becoming something of a folk hero in some circles. Other friends (or former friends) of the university canceled their pledges. I appeared on several local television shows, once with the campus rabbi, who understandably did not agree with the student editors' decision or mine. Predictably, in such times of superheated controversy, there were bomb threats, all proving to be fake, but distracting nonetheless. It is sobering to be reminded, especially in emotional times of crisis, how close to the surface of civilization are violent impulses.

My trustees and I worked together to try to calm the uproar, in the Jewish community especially. One of the most important organizations in Miami is the Greater Miami Jewish Federation. Several of our trustees were active leaders of the federation. They arranged for me to meet with appropriate federation leaders. I proposed trying to write a joint statement with the executive director of the federation, but after the exchange of several drafts, the exercise proved futile. The federation decided that any joint statement at that stage might be interpreted as support for the publication of the advertisement. I respected the decision, even though I was disappointed. The controversy boiled along day by day. Mail, pro and con, flooded my office.

With fortunate timing, the annual meeting and retreat of the board of trustees took place on April 22 and 23, 1994. That meeting had become an important event over the years. It was a combination of the usual business items of an annual meeting, election of officers, and the like, and consideration of the next five-year iteration of the university's strategic plan. For years, the trustees had held this event outside of Miami to avoid distraction. Not surprisingly, in 1994, we spent much of our time discussing the Holocaust advertisement controversy. By then, everyone knew the basic facts, and no one was without an opinion. In twenty years, it was the liveliest of all those trustee meetings, even some having to do with football. With key Jewish leaders of the board, I had been preparing for the meeting in hopes of fashioning a constructive response and maybe some closure. After much debate, the board adopted this statement:

> As trustees of the University of Miami, we deeply regret the pain and anguish caused in our community by the decision of the student editors of *The Miami Hurricane* to publish an advertisement questioning certain evidence of the Holocaust.
>
> No one can underestimate the horrors of the Holocaust, the most methodical program of mass genocide in human history. The suffering of Jews, especially, but others also, is well documented and irrefutable. It must always be remembered. It must never be repeated.
>
> Our president, Edward T. Foote II, found the advertisement totally inappropriate, as we do. He would not have published it as a student editor, but allowed it as president. His rationale was that students should be allowed the latitude to make such decisions.
>
> Even those in disagreement with President Foote respect his integrity on this issue. It is one of the most difficult decisions of his tenure as president. He believes that great universities must take the lead in remembrance of the past so critical to preventing tragedies of the future. We agree.
>
> We also reaffirm the premise that freedom of thought and expression must be protected, especially at a university. As trustees we want to make it clear that:
>
> - We unequivocally reject the content of the advertisement in the student newspaper and its implicit message of hate.
> - While there is difference of opinion among trustees over the decision of the president not to overrule the student editors, no one on the board questions the commitment of Tad Foote to human rights and dignity. He is a champion of equality and justice. Few are more pained than he by the hurt caused by this issue. The Board of Trustees expresses without reservation its full confidence in President Foote and his leadership.
> - We endorse the president's efforts already underway to develop new guidelines for advertisements in student publications according to

accepted standards of media ethics and professionalism. Hateful and misleading advertisements should be rejected.

- From adversity there is opportunity to learn and grow. While today the
issue may be the Holocaust, tomorrow it may be an extremist perspective
of a different nature. No group has a monopoly on hate. The university will
continue to build on its existing programs and expand the teaching of the
Holocaust.

We are proud of the University of Miami and its 68-year tradition of service
to our community. As trustees, we must help prevent another Holocaust
through education, compassion, and understanding. We rededicate ourselves
not only to the building of a great American university, but also to the building of a great community.

This statement appeared April 24, 1994, in the *Miami Herald* (Board of
Trustees, 1994). On April 26, 1994, Charles E. Cobb, the chair of the board
of trustees, issued an additional statement:

On behalf of the Board of Trustees, I emphasize again that academic freedom, including especially for student editors, will be treasured and defended
at the University of Miami. Regrettably, some students mistakenly interpreted the trustees' April 24th statement concerning the Holocaust advertisement that appeared in *The Miami Hurricane* to suggest something less
than full editorial freedom for our student editors. The trustees' statement
did "endorse the president's efforts already underway to develop new guidelines for advertisements in student publications according to the acceptable
standards of media ethics and professionalism. Hateful and misleading advertisements should be rejected." Students, members of the faculty, and administrators during the summer will conduct the review. The trustees *did not*
even consider, much less mention, censorship or prior approval of editorial
discretion. The trustees' statement reaffirmed "the premise that freedom of
thought and expression must be protected, especially at a university."

Cobb defended academic freedom but endorsed "new guidelines" for
advertisements in the student newspapers. Understandably, he was trying
to find a sensible line between academic freedom and a reasonable policy
concerning what should be published as an advertisement in the student
newspaper. Perhaps predictably, four student editors resigned from the staff
of the *Hurricane* to protest this review of their advertising policy. Later,
three returned. (In late April, there came from the German High Court an
ironic counterpoint. The court limited the free speech of neo-Nazis who had
denied the Holocaust.)

By May, the university was refocusing on the end of the academic year,
approaching commencement and the blessed closure of approaching summer. The steady stream of letters slowed. I had answered every letter,

believing in the process of full communication during a time of emotional crisis. As is supposed to happen on a university campus, people who had taken extreme views earlier at least had begun to understand why those opposed disagreed. The board of student publications, led by students, revised the guidelines for advertising, bringing them into conformity with generally accepted standards in the media. At least twice since then, student editors have turned down similar advertisements.

Presidential Reflections

Freedom of thought and speech on a campus is nearly sacred, and it should be. Of all the places where ideas should be paramount, universities are at the top. If learned professors and learning students cannot freely test each other, pursue truth uncensored, disagree, criticize, accept or reject, then all of us in human society are the losers. As I tried to reflect in my statement issued at the height of the controversy, freedom of thought and speech provide the foundation for human understanding, including formal education. But freedom must be considered in its various contexts. Although everyone on a campus is free to think, believe, and speak, consequences vary depending on the circumstances. As at Hyde Park in London, one is free to stand on a stump and deliver his or her views on politics, religion, and anything else. A faculty member, especially if tenured, is famously free to follow his or her scholarship where it may lead, whether the conclusion be acceptable to the majority or a radical departure from accepted dogma. Once published, however, the author's ideas are fair game for all concerned, and the resulting debates within the academy are notorious for their intensity and, occasionally, ferocity. A faculty member has great freedom in the classroom to teach as he or she will. But students do not have freedom in that same classroom to follow their own inquiries independent of the guidelines of the course. If the instructor assigns a paper on Chaucer, the student may not demur and write about Shakespeare without permission for the change.

Student publications have always occupied an interesting corner of the area of academic freedom. Although most universities would not exercise prior review, there are certain subtle constraints, at least practically speaking. Some student newspapers are entirely independent. Others are governed by a board of the kind that exists at the University of Miami, comprising students, faculty members, and administrators. The board is primarily responsible for setting policy and appointing the student editors.

Advertisements in a student newspaper present an additional set of issues because they reflect not necessarily the views of the editors but of the paying advertiser. It was that distinction that divided many who were critical of the decision to run the advertisement. Our students had been duped, some said, into promoting a message of hate that they themselves rejected, all in the name of freedom of expression. To me, it was a distinction without significant difference. The right to be preserved is one of editorial choice. It is exercised daily in newspapers throughout the world, including student newspapers. It is not only the right to judge an editorial, an op-ed piece, or letter to the editor, deciding which should run and which should not. It is also the right to determine what advertisements shall run under what policies.

The students' right to make that decision should be preserved on a university campus. The proposition that freedom of expression will ultimately lead toward the greatest truth was richly fulfilled during our Holocaust controversy. As the drama unfolded, the campus sprang alive, stimulating intense interest. There were articles in the student newspaper, editorials and letters to the editor of all kinds, demonstrations, a forum, a program with Holocaust survivors, countless informal discussions, and many meetings around the community. Smith's lame pronouncements and misleading questions were discussed, refuted, and rejected, which is as the system should work with falsehoods. I doubt that anyone who lived through those several weeks of emotional turmoil will ever forget the lessons learned, about freedom and the Holocaust, but also about themselves and others.

Universities are hardy institutions. Built on freedom, learning, dreams, and hope, they enjoy deep and strong foundations. Thus it is that challenges to one of these foundational pillars raise special concerns. Academic freedom is not a hollow mantra of those seeking protection for the wrong things. It is at the core of academic life. No attack on a university holds more threat because academic freedom sustains all that we do in higher education. It is the oxygen of inquiry. It was at the heart of our dispute over the Holocaust.

Those who opposed the right of students to run the ad did so out of concern that the existence of the Holocaust would suffer potential distortion. They feared that allowing Smith to purchase the advertisement demeaned the newspaper even as it misled readers into misunderstanding a ghastly chapter in human history. An underlying theme was that the university itself was somehow involved in this cruel hoax. In the name of freedom, many exclaimed, the university had deliberately, or at least passively, contributed to the dissemination of misinformation. The passion that shines from all the letters, telephone calls, and speeches in opposition to publication of the advertisement was directed against not only Smith but also those who allowed the university to be so "compromised."

In retrospect, most of us concede that at best the call was close. There is in fact a difference between a student article or editorial and an advertisement. The first must be protected at all costs, at least within the usual bounds of freedom of the media, whereas the second presents additional complexities. The ideas expressed are not necessarily those of students, as in Smith's case, but of people outside the university. Such people may have nothing to do with the university or even wish it harm. Why, then, should their ability to be misleading be protected? Why should students be allowed to make such a damaging choice?

These questions, at the heart of the Holocaust advertisement dispute, are also at the heart of the university itself. Freedom is tested most powerfully when it cloaks the idea we hate. Most people hated Smith's message, but the student editors decided for their own reasons to let the advertisement run, saying at the same time that they joined others in disputing the theme of the advertisement. They believed that counteropinions would arise, as indeed they did, and that the ultimate result would be readers and others who learned a great deal about a desperately sorry period in history. It was the freedom to make such a decision that was at stake. It is a freedom as precious as it was controversial.

The controversy also highlighted the importance of a concerned, active board of trustees. Our trustees acted as interpreter between the university and its community and also as defender. Our Jewish trustees in particular sustained significant criticism. Although inevitably I had become the lightning rod, the board of trustees itself assumed responsibility for the university's policies, including especially its policy of freedom of expression. I doubt that the university would have emerged as strong, resilient, and unharmed as it did without the quiet leadership of key trustees.

Although many of the events during the Holocaust advertisement controversy remain painful years later, more than a little good emerged from the intense, sometimes angry exchanges. First, the most visible of our disaffected friends, the one who canceled his pledge for $2 million, rethought his action, reinstated the pledge, and remains to this day a good friend of the university. Of even more lasting significance will be the culmination of a dream long held by many of us. Because of the significant Jewish population in Miami and the community's and university's many ties with Israel, our strategic planning had long envisioned creation of a Center for Judaic Studies. Indeed, we were working on that project when the controversy erupted. We put it aside until things had cooled. Many of the same people who had played leadership roles in the Holocaust controversy became even closer to the university and took the lead in the creation of a Judaic studies center. Principal among them are the former chair of the board and his wife, whose magnificent financial commitment stimulated many others and made possible the creation of the Sue and Leonard Miller Center for Contemporary Judaic Studies. It should not surprise us that many critics of the Holocaust advertisement decision have supported the Miller Center, believing now, even more than before, that the best protection against another such human tragedy is freedom and knowledge.

References

Board of Trustees, University of Miami. "UM Trustees: Ad Was Inappropriate." *Miami Herald,* Ap. 24, 1994, section C, p. 5, col. 2, 39 words.

Cobb, C. E. [statement]. *Miami Herald,* Apr. 26, 1994, p. 1B.

Gonzalez, A. M., and Muhs, A. "UM Paper Accepts Ad Questioning Holocaust." *Miami Herald,* Apr. 9, 1994, section B, p. 1.
Teitelbaum, A. N. "The Holocaust Happened." *Miami Herald,* April 12, 1994, section A, p. 9.

EDWARD T. FOOTE II *was president of the University of Miami from 1981 to 2001 and chancellor from 2001 to 2003.*

*In her first month in office, a president learns of charges
of racial discrimination in the university's intercollegiate
athletic program to which she must respond at the same
time as she is learning her way around campus and
establishing herself in the community.*

Leading a University During Controversy: Challenges Faced by a New President

Judy Genshaft, Jack Wheat

Except for founding presidents, new university presidents are creatures of inheritance. As job candidates, they carefully assess the university, looking for strengths on which to build and conducting environmental scans to detect challenges and problems. Once on the job, they can expect the satisfaction of discovering institutional potential of which they had been unaware, but they will also encounter unexpected challenges. The certainty of unanticipated challenge means effective presidents must believe every crisis and every dilemma bring opportunities for the president to emerge as a stronger leader and the institution as a stronger university. It also means new presidents should come into the job with personal values that support their visions and aspirations for the institution.

I became the sixth president of the University of South Florida (USF) in July 2000. Since its opening forty-three years ago, the university has rapidly emerged as a major public research university with more than forty-one thousand students, four campuses, a maturing academic medical center, and a prime location in the vast, powerful metropolitan area of Tampa Bay, within the growing state of Florida. USF had already established programs of national distinction, and I could clearly see the young institution's potential. There were extraordinarily strong programs whose achievements were just becoming recognized and others that were poised to take off.

One month after assuming the presidency of USF, I received my first piece of information about a situation that would soon mushroom into a major controversy: an allegation of racial discrimination and retaliation

NEW DIRECTIONS FOR HIGHER EDUCATION, no. 128, Winter 2004 © Wiley Periodicals, Inc.

47

against an African American female student in intercollegiate athletics. The number of allegations within the athletic department would grow over time, and resolution of the controversy would take more than a year.

Much of what was learned in dealing with this case has particular relevance for new presidents. Leading an institution through controversy requires more than demonstrated academic leadership and the administrative, fundraising, and political skills that typically are the focus of presidential searches. Fundamental to an effective presidency is a strong sense of academic and ethical principle, an understanding of the importance of all institutional constituencies to the university's success, a deep comprehension of the symbolic nature of the presidency, and a dogged determination to shepherd the university through the controversy not only intact but strengthened.

The following is a condensed version of the facts of the USF women's basketball case. Due to editorial considerations, I do not attempt to present every detail or viewpoint regarding the facts of this complex matter.

USF Women's Basketball Litigation: A Case Study

This is a case about the convergence of two potentially explosive issues of modern university life—race and athletics—into one crisis. When I assumed my duties as president, I was unaware of the events that had already occurred, that would further unfold, and that would occupy a prominent place during the first year of my presidency.

In July 2000, the university had many athletic successes to celebrate. Under the leadership of its athletic director of fifteen years, the university had become a founding member of the newly formed "Conference USA." The university's teams had won sixty-three conference championships in men's and women's sports. Out of the eighteen sports governed by the National Collegiate Athletic Association (NCAA), the only one not yet competing in Division IA was the new football team, but that, too, was an astounding institutional triumph. USF athletics faced the same financial issues as major programs at most other universities. But from the information immediately available to me as a new president, there were no signs that the athletic department was a trouble spot.

First impressions are not always correct. As it turned out, even before I became a candidate for the USF presidency, allegations of racial discrimination in the women's basketball program had begun to surface.

Beginnings of a Controversy

Between January and March 1999, an associate athletic director heard complaints of racial discrimination in the women's athletic program. Most came from African American members of the team and a few from program staff and from a student's mother. Those complaints included allegations of racial slurs by the white female head coach of the women's basketball team, the coach's white boyfriend, and a white male assistant coach; segregation of black and white players in room assignments on trips; white players receiving more playing opportunities; and a high turnover of African American players—all allegations the coach denied. The associate athletic director, an African American man, reported the complaints to the athletic director.

The athletic director, a white man, asked the associate athletic director to conduct an internal departmental inquiry of the allegations. The athletic director had the option to forward the matter to the university's Equal Opportunity Affairs (EOA) office. This was, under existing university policy, a judgment call for the athletic director to make, but as events unfolded it became clear that referral to the EOA office would have spared the athletic department, its director, and in point of fact, the university much criticism.

After receiving the assignment to investigate the complaints, the associate athletic director provided a report to the athletic director concluding that there were issues of "racial insensitivity," team dynamics, and coach-team communication. The associate athletic director later contended that the athletic director suggested that he soften his findings and he complied, fearing for his job. The athletic director vehemently denied this allegation. This factual dispute between the athletic director and the associate athletic director was never resolved during the controversy.

The athletic director proceeded with efforts to resolve the issues within the department. He held one-on-one counseling sessions with the coach, gave her a negative evaluation, and directed her to go through sensitivity training. The coach, in turn, directed the entire team to go through the sensitivity training. The athletic director closely monitored the women's basketball program, frequently attending practices and games to observe the dynamics. As the 1999–2000 season progressed, it appeared that the situation was resolved.

But when the 1999–2000 season ended in March 2000, conflict between the coach and some African American players resumed. The coach dismissed a player from the team—the player who had complained earlier—after an incident that occurred on the team bus. The coach stated that her decision was based on the player's disrespectful behavior. Affidavits filed by the coach, an assistant coach, and some players stated that the head coach treated the dismissed player no differently than other team members, that the coach tried to improve the relationship but the student-athlete persisted in creating turmoil, and that the student-athlete manifested a bad attitude and tried to instigate confrontation with the coaches.

The athletic director supported the coach's decision to remove the player from the team, considering the need for respect from the players essential to successfully coaching the team. However, the athletic director insisted that the player's scholarship remain in effect—perhaps as a concession to the history of difficulty between the player and the coach. The player was not satisfied with this, and in April 1999, she filed an official university retaliation complaint for being removed from the team. This triggered an official university EOA investigation.

President Learns of the Controversy

My first exposure to the allegations came in August 2000, only one month after I began my job as university president. I was not informed that the routine processes of the university had begun to review the allegations or that a local attorney known for conducting high-profile federal discrimination litigation had recently made a detailed public records request. Instead, I learned of the controversy when meeting with the associate athletic director who conducted the internal athletic department review. The meeting was at his request, and as a new president, I was eager to establish a culture of openness at USF. I listened attentively to the associate athletic director as he expressed concern that his job was to be eliminated. He felt that the investigation he had conducted might be the cause of the loss of his position. He offered to give me a copy of his report, but I assured him that I believed his concerns were sincere and that the issue would be investigated by EOA. Later, I informed senior administrators of the conversation and asked them to look into allegations of an improperly handled discrimination investigation and the associate athletic director's fears regarding his job. They found that the grant that was paying his salary would soon expire but that there was a position in another division of the university for which he would be suited. Ultimately, he was transferred to another department. It was not clear to me when I met with the associate athletic director—or even today—that he wanted any other action from me as USF's president. I sincerely believed that my facilitation of his transfer to another department was exactly what he hoped would be accomplished by our meeting. Within weeks, routine processes turned into public controversy when the student-athlete filed a federal lawsuit alleging illegal discrimination and retaliation. Suddenly, the university was prominent in newspaper headlines such as "Racism Coverup Alleged at USF" (Johnston, 2001), "USF Coach Is Accused of Bias" (Mills, English, and Fry, 2000), and "Already Tested, USF President Is Inaugurated Today" (Klein, 2001).

Developing a Plan of Action

I was fortunate as a new president to have an excellent general counsel and administrative team to consult with. Because there were conflicting versions of events, we recognized that the most urgent imperative was to move quickly to objectively assess the matter. I was determined to commission a thorough, unrestricted independent inquiry. After considering concerns that an outside inquiry might undermine the university's legal defense and disrupt the athletic program, I still believed that the overwhelming consideration was the community's and public's confidence in USF's integrity. I consulted with the chancellor of the state university system, the chair of the board of regents, my administrative team, faculty and community leaders, and institutional friends regarding my plan. There was widespread support for such an objective review, and the advice I received was to select a person of outstanding reputation and stature. After further consultation regarding potential candidates, I retained one of the state and nation's most distinguished jurists, Judge Joseph Hatchett. Hatchett was the first African American justice of the Florida Supreme Court and later served as a U.S. Circuit Judge and then Chief of the U.S. Eleventh Circuit Court of Appeals, which adjudicated appeals cases from throughout the Southeast. One of the nation's authorities on civil rights law, he had retired from the bench and was in private practice. He met with me and my general counsel, reviewed available information, and came back with a proposal to assess this complex situation.

He proposed to review the university's policies and procedures for dealing with allegations of racial discrimination, an approach that would include but not be limited to the women's basketball case. He said his review should continue until after resolution of the EOA investigation so that he could assess that process in action. All of his proposals were readily agreed to without hesitation.

The university was now involved in three separate processes: federal litigation, the university EOA investigation, and the Hatchett review. The processes were separate, but they dealt with overlapping allegations. The greatest disadvantage of this approach was confusion among reporters, their readers and listeners, and anyone who did not closely follow the details of the controversy. The issue became even larger as national media, including the Bryant Gumbel program *Real Sports* on HBO, profiled the case. With national media attention, the issue began to reverberate through our athletic conference, Conference USA. As a brand new president, I had to explain to my colleague presidents what the case was about and how I was dealing with it. They assured me that issues in athletics were common, and although generally sympathetic, they often said, "I'm glad it is you and not me dealing with this!"

Whereas the EOA investigation proceeded quietly, federal litigation provided daily fodder for a media frenzy. Over a period of months, the attorney representing the student-athlete added plaintiff after plaintiff, most of them members or former members of the women's basketball team and a few former staff. Each new suit made essentially the same allegations: that the university's women's basketball coach had discriminated against an African American player and segregated the team in hotel rooms while traveling, at meals, and at practices. Each time, the attorney would call a press conference and, on the day before the press conference, release the details as an "exclusive" to one of the newspapers. This ensured a large media turnout at his press conference, thereby producing two days of high-profile news coverage for one event. Constant repetition of the same allegations was among the most frustrating aspects of this situation. The media relations staff and I attempted to explain the three separate processes and the status of each. But these efforts were often made moot by intense competition among news organizations and their limited time and space for analyzing and reporting on the case. My most effective strategy was to continue with the fast-paced activities of a new president and to take advantage of the community's interest in the new leader to promote my values, to laud the achievements of the university, and to set a new direction. I gave speeches on the university's role in the community; economic development; the university's extensive engagement in nationally relevant research, scholarship, and creative work; and the first "State of the University Address." I was focused on successful completion of the university's capital campaign. I met with faculty, staff, and student leaders and civic and corporate leaders; worked at building political coalitions to protect the university's interests in statewide reorganization efforts for higher education governance; and began planning the presidential inauguration for February 2001. So the series of stories focusing on the women's basketball program was tempered by articles and television coverage indicating a new president propelling the university forward on many fronts. Clearly, the public recognized that I inherited this controversy, but attention was still focused on me and how I would resolve the matter.

Preparing for and Evaluating the Reports

While awaiting an EOA finding, I worked with other administrators to develop strategies for a quick response to whatever the EOA reported. With such divided opinion, the EOA finding, whatever it might be, would draw extensive attention and action in the form of an implementation plan, and public response would still need to occur. In late October 2000, the EOA's findings were released. They concluded there was reasonable cause to believe that the coach had engaged in retaliation. After an appeal by the coach (which upheld the first decision), the athletic director announced the dismissal of the women's basketball coach, reinstatement of the student-athlete to the team, and appointment of the interim coach as head coach. (The coach later sued the university for reinstatement; the University of South Florida won the case.) In mid-January 2001, Judge Hatchett (2001) completed his report. He concluded that the primary problem stemmed from the policy that authorized EOA to investigate a racial discrimination claim only if an affected department requested it or a student, faculty, or staff member filed a formal complaint.

As a matter of judgment, he wrote, the athletic director or associate athletic director should have sought EOA involvement early in the case, and had either done so, it likely could have been resolved satisfactorily through outside mediators' help in identifying issues and correcting them. But the judge pointed out that the athletic director had acted within university policy. He noted that several years earlier, USF had begun requiring that all complaints of sexual harassment be reported to EOA and recommended the same policy for complaints of racial discrimination. He recommended eliminating the policy restricting EOA investigations to formal complaints, saying it would often be more helpful for the EOA office to become involved as soon as informal complaints occurred. He also recommended a number of procedural changes, such as revising timetables for various steps in the complaint, investigation, and appeals processes.

Organizational Changes and Improvements

As I lived through daily manifestations of the controversy, I realized that a stronger, more coherent administrative structure was necessary for diversity and equal opportunity actions. I found that the various offices dealing with diversity issues were scattered throughout the campus and reported to different vice presidents and that there was no central committee or person to bring these programs together to function as a cohesive whole. The diversity education unit was lodged in academic affairs, and the EOA was housed at a lower level in the budgets and human resources division. Communication between the two units was erratic. There was no mechanism to provide the president and provost with an overall picture of the state of diversity at USF or ensure they were aware of compliance issues.

During the fall term, I worked closely with the provost and other members of my staff as we developed several reorganization models. As a new president unfamiliar with the environment at the university, I was informed by the understanding and experiences of my staff, many of whom had been at USF for several years. I relied on them to give me an understanding of the community dynamics and history in the area of race relations. When the Hatchett report was released, I was prepared to announce our acceptance of all of his recommendations. Effective immediately, all racial discrimination complaints had to be reported to the EOA. The provost and I rolled out a plan to reorganize diversity and equal opportunity operations into a new, high-profile Diversity and Equal Opportunity Office, and the associate vice president for diversity and equal opportunity would be a member of the president's staff and regularly report to the president on the state of diversity and equal opportunity compliance issues. As an associate vice president, the officer would report daily to the provost to ensure that diversity operations received the consistent monitoring they needed and to integrate that function into the division of the university with the most employees, biggest budgets, and most contact with students. We established a task force to develop the numerous procedural changes required to complete implementation of the Hatchett report.

We also focused efforts on assuring our constituencies that USF was a diverse and welcoming environment. The provost developed a faculty academic enhancement program designed to encourage the hiring of minority faculty. We recruited an outstanding associate vice president for enrollment planning and management who brought exciting strategies for increasing minority recruitment and retention to the university. We began working closely with advisory groups like the Status of Women Committee, the Latino Advisory Committee, and the Committee on Black Affairs to understand their concerns.

Changes in the Athletic Department

With the university's internal and external reviews completed and reform actions under way, it was time to assess the effects of the crisis on the athletic department. I knew the department's challenges included moving past the race controversy and the development of modern management systems with the accountabilities essential for a president to ensure institutional control of a program with multimillion dollar budgets, numerous revenue streams, increasing competitive pressures, hundreds of student-athletes, increasingly supportive and involved boosters, and rising NCAA standards. All of these elements contribute to the success of well-managed athletic programs with strong institutional oversight.

Although grateful for the athletic director's contributions to our university, I soon concluded that the program had progressed to a level where it needed new leadership and management approaches. I was concerned that the controversy had affected the athletic director's ability to effectively lead the department. Whereas many in athletics were loyal to him, the wider university and community had less confidence after the judgment calls he made on this case were held up to such intense public scrutiny. I discussed resignation with him, and ultimately, at my request, the athletic director resigned in early March 2001. The university honored a provision in his employment contract guaranteeing his level of income for two years. Unfortunately, the process turned more awkward and publicly acrimonious than I expected. Although there was considerable external pressure for a change in leadership of the athletic department, internal staff was largely loyal to the athletic director. I was convinced that the university needed a fresh start to rise above the controversy, and it fell to me to plead that case to those who questioned the departure of the athletic director. I held long and emotional meetings with coaches, the athletic staff, and leaders of the booster organization, listening to concerns, explaining the decision, and assuring them of our commitment to excellent athletics at USF.

Before beginning the search for a new athletic director, I developed a strategy for learning about departmental functioning and finances. Rather than name an interim director, I appointed a management committee of two associate athletic directors and the university's executive vice president. I next commissioned a thorough management review by a national sports consulting firm, whose report noted a lack of staff diversity; significant financial challenges; deficient facilities and technology for such a large and ambitious program; and a need to integrate the athletic department into general university operations to strengthen compliance oversight, improve financial management, marketing, and fundraising, and strengthen the university experience for student-athletes. The report said USF needed an athletic director of great stature who could effectively raise money, strengthen marketing, bring new people into the fold of USF supporters, and provide a national presence for the program. It recommended a management structure that included an athletic director who would provide general oversight and strengthen the program's external credibility and a strong deputy director for daily internal administration. Already on staff at USF was Lee Roy Selmon. Inducted into the College Football Hall of Fame for his feats at the University of Oklahoma, the first Tampa Bay Buccaneer inducted into the Pro Football Hall of Fame, and active in civic affairs, Selmon is such an icon in Tampa Bay, particularly in the African American community, that a major expressway is named for him. He had joined USF in the 1990s as associate athletic director to help with the startup of the football program. Consultants advised that a search could find no more suitable candidate and recommended Selmon as athletic director. After consulting with various constituent groups, including the university search committee charged with identifying candidates, and finding that Selmon enjoyed their admiration and confidence, I made the appointment and we began implementation of the various management recommendations.

As the university implemented its reorganization, the ongoing federal litigation (ultimately settled by the parties) had a steadily diminishing effect. The women's basketball team, under leadership of its new coach, a Latino, rebuilt more quickly than anyone had hoped. No quick fixes presented themselves for other challenges, but under the leadership of Selmon and fellow university administrators, integration of the department's financial, marketing, fundraising, and academic support functions into university-wide systems began, a process that will continue as the university implements state-of-the-art financial and records management systems. I considered it important to demonstrate my commitment to athletics through my presence at many events and through enthusiastic involvement in the efforts to raise private funding and obtain other financing for an impressive athletic facility that will improve national competitiveness and improve the facilities and profile of men's and women's sports.

Lessons Learned

The lessons learned from this experience can be broadly summed up in the following five statements.

1. The Importance of a Well-Defined Sense of Academic and Ethical Values. I came to USF with a strong personal commitment to diversity in the sense that I aspired to create an open environment where all would feel welcomed. I took steps to create a diverse environment early on, such as the composition of my senior advisors. My cabinet included more than 50 percent women and minorities, and in making my first appointment, the position of provost and vice president for academic affairs, I turned to the dean of the College of Arts and Sciences, a distinguished African American sociologist who had done groundbreaking work on race and ethnicity in Syracuse, New York, and Tampa, and who had previously served USF as special assistant to the president, with minority affairs one of his major assignments. When I made the appointment, I did not realize how fortuitous the decision would be. But soon, as a newcomer, I would be relying on him, his knowledge of the university and community, and his expertise in issues of race and equity to help the university through a controversy that stirred deep emotions and threatened to become extremely polarizing.

My past experience had not tested my values on diversity in the way that the controversy at USF would test them. I found that the African American community both within the university and external to it were nursing wounds from past history and that the controversy in athletics touched nerves of wounds that were unhealed. I saw the effect this had on public confidence in the university and on morale. And I emerged from the controversy at my university with a deeply held belief that the actions of a university president set the tone for how the institution is perceived on diversity issues. For me, diversity enriches the educational experience, and to this day I try to communicate that throughout our institution. I focus attention on all students, including minority students, and on faculty recruitment strategies, retention efforts, graduation rates, and recognition events. The USF seal carries the motto, "Truth and Wisdom"; I consider that motto as my charge. The president is the standard bearer for the academic and ethical principles of the institution. In the face of controversy, despite public pressure or what is politically expedient, the president must be focused on what is right and must not be swayed.

2. Importance of an Objective View. In retrospect, I believe my most significant response was moving quickly to obtain an outside reviewer of stature and expertise. Judge Hatchett's approach gave us an extraordinary opportunity to convert a crisis in one corner of the university into a transformational process for the entire institution. Having an objective analysis, even where fault may be found, gave me credibility as a leader who was willing to examine the institution and who valued protecting its integrity. Ultimately, this enhanced the perception of the university among many of its constituencies.

I came to the decision to seek Judge Hatchett's advice after pursuing another important strategy: consultation. I am a firm believer in seeking many viewpoints before reaching a decision. I spoke with faculty, staff, students, community members, civic groups, and my senior staff. I heard differing opinions, but my decision-making ability was enriched by knowing what the various constituencies and individuals thought about the controversy.

3. Understanding and Reaching All Constituencies. A president's enthusiastic engagement in activities to produce and highlight achievements throughout the institution are critical to coming through a controversy. It is the president's duty to offer a perspective. Although there may be issues affecting one area of the university, there is so much more of the story to tell. In our case, headlines about problems in the athletics department were counterbalanced by reports such as the university's exceeding the goal of its capital campaign by 20 percent, experiencing one of the nation's fastest-rising rates of external research funding, increasing international recognition of USF's eminence in fields such as Alzheimer's research, construction programs of unprecedented scale, winning a major political battle in the statewide reorganization of education governance, rising enrollment and student qualifications, successful implementation of a new governance system that gave USF its first institutional board of trustees, and development of the university's most strategic and performance-based comprehensive plan ever. And despite headlines and news coverage about the athletic department's problems, individual athletic teams achieved increasing national recognition.

In addition to speaking opportunities, new presidents should focus on identifying and establishing ties with highly respected, influential, and knowledgeable people in the community who love the university, understand its mission, and have an interest in the institution's success. It is through one-on-one relationships that the president's voice and message are able to reverberate through and reach the larger community in a personal way that leads to confidence. Finally, the internal constituency cannot be ignored. By appointing a highly respected, eminently qualified provost and vice president for academic affairs and by working with him throughout the controversy to stress our commitment as a team to addressing the controversy, we were able to restore confidence in the university. Together we involved diverse student groups, newspapers, advisory groups, governance groups such as the faculty senate, and others in discussion of the controversy, and we assured them of our commitment to diversity.

4. Role of the Media. The women's basketball case at USF highlighted institutional shortcomings, but the controversy was amplified, distorted, and complicated by intensive media coverage. The Tampa Bay region is among the nation's most competitive media markets and one of the few remaining metropolitan areas with intense circulation and status rivalries between two big-city daily newspapers. Moreover, Florida has expansive public records ("sunshine") laws. With few exceptions, when a reporter or any citizen requests records, the university must provide the documents. In a case as complex as this one, reporters requesting documents relating to some subject often find hundreds of pages of material on their desks—far more than they could possibly read, analyze, and place in context under the deadlines they face.

My administrative team and I spent much time with reporters reviewing the sequences of events and other public information. Still, there was much scattershot reporting and accusations that were unaccompanied by available information that refuted them. Presidents must recognize and accept that media, both broadcast and print, by their nature produce unstructured and incomplete public debate of institutional issues, and the resulting impressions can have enormous consequences. Administrators can spare themselves a great deal of personal frustration by recognizing and accepting that media are governed by different objectives and follow different rules from the institutions they cover. Whereas news organizations work to produce conclusive stories on a daily basis, the institutions they cover strive to follow deliberate processes to reach conclusions that they know are valid and are confident will withstand administrative and legal challenges. A president must establish an effective media relations function within the university to ensure that the university message is heard. I charged our media representatives to remain responsive to media inquiries while imparting the message that the institution would review the matter and address it in a deliberate and careful manner. On many days the challenge was finding the most artful way to say, "We have high standards of behavior. We are investigating, and when we have collected and reviewed all the facts, we will thoroughly report our conclusions and take any necessary corrective actions."

The president must play a role in shaping the message of the university in a controversy. It is critical to behave in a consistent, strong manner, always clarifying the essential message and values that you hold for the university. My messages about my vision and plans for USF were usually followed by essential discussions on the importance of diversity and equal opportunity, due process, and strong athletic programs. Critical to a new president's credibility is the ability to display command of the facts and to impart the plan for resolving the controversy. Because of the intense media scrutiny surrounding the controversy, my staff and I sought out media workshops to enhance presentation skills. My extensive personal appearances gave USF an opportunity to reach out to the community and civic leaders. This gave these opinion leaders the information they needed to question the deluge of information presented by the media. Presidents should recognize the nature of contemporary media and their effect on perceptions about themselves and their institutions. News coverage may identify a controversy, but it can be notoriously inaccurate in identifying the problem itself and contributing factors. Honest, proactive media relations promote consistent institutional messages and limit opportunities for damaging contradictions.

5. Dogged Determination to Move the Institution Forward. The president must remain fully engaged in achieving institutional goals in all areas and develop an administrative team that can keep units of the institution on track. As we reorganized the EOA and diversity offices and changed the direction and leadership of the athletics department, I found that my chief duty as president was the reinforcement of my vision for USF and my insistence that we press forward despite the controversy we were engaged in. Presidents, almost by definition, must multitask. The president must keep one eye on achieving institutional goals even while engaged in a controversy. When the controversy is over, people may not recall it well, but one can be assured they will want to know what achievements, gains, or strides the institution has made under this president's leadership. As controversy fades, my legacy as president will be based on the institutional goals achieved.

I have made diversity issues a part of institutional planning, developed minority programs, and tried to instill in my staff the understanding that I want diversity to be a part of our institutional value system. In this era of evaluation and accountability, I know we will be judged on our hiring, student retention, and institutional climate. Whether an institutional crisis involves diversity or some other issue, I know it is my job to keep our institution focused on solving problems of substance and making and promoting achievements of substance. The certainty of unanticipated challenge means that effective presidents must believe that every crisis and every dilemma bring opportunities for the president to emerge as a stronger leader and the institution as a stronger university.

Conclusion

Race issues and issues related to athletic programs generate their share of controversy in today's universities. These issues are magnets for extensive media coverage and hold high public interest. As a new president, I endured a challenge that combined these two issues and that challenged my leadership skills and my value system in an intense context. In the end, the events that began in the athletic department propelled significant and continuing university-wide enhancement of systems for encouraging diversity and ensuring equal opportunity and fair treatment for all members of the university.

As the new policy requiring mandatory reporting of all claims of racial discrimination was implemented, general confidence among minority members of the university in the process appeared to increase. The university recruited a highly effective head of diversity and equal opportunity operations who has focused on rebuilding the university's compliance operation and on diversity education. She has made inroads to areas of the universities and groups of students, faculty, and staff that previously had not dealt with diversity and equal opportunity offices. I now have regular meetings with minority advocacy groups, and the meetings are both collegial and productive. The university is examining options for streamlining the committee structure for diversity and equity issues to make possible more timely review of arising issues and possible policy changes.

The student-athlete who filed the initial complaint and lawsuit ultimately graduated from the university. In fact, after her reinstatement to the team, she played for the new coach during her senior year at USF. The long-time athletic director who resigned from USF has resumed his career on the staff of a different major university. The women's basketball coach appealed her dismissal through the state administrative appeals process and was denied reinstatement. She also appealed the decision to state court, and that decision was pending at the time of this chapter's publication.

Throughout the controversy, there were many people who believed that our minority, particularly African American, enrollment would plummet. But university recruiters found ways to let prospective minority students know that USF is a welcoming place where they could achieve and excel. Despite early concerns regarding the effect of the controversy on enrollment, USF experienced a 57 percent increase in enrollment of minorities attending college for the first time between 2000 and 2003 and a 25 percent increase in total minority enrollment during the same period. I attribute these gains in part to the organizational changes we made as part of our efforts to focus on being viewed as a diverse and welcoming environment despite the controversy in athletics.

As do all universities with major athletic programs, USF faces long-term challenges of ensuring financial soundness, academic achievement, diversity, and sportsmanship. But I am confident that the university's athletic programs, and the university, will continue to grow and excel in strategic directions. The experiences I encountered as a new president leading my university through this controversy tested me, but they also confirmed for me that principle and determination are essential to leadership.

References

Hatchett, J. "Investigation Involving Charges of Racial Discrimination in the Woman's Basketball Program in 1999," January, 2001.

Johnston, J. "Racism Coverup Alleged at USF." *Tampa Tribune,* March 2, 2001, nation/world section, p. 1.

Klein, Barry. "Already Tested, USF President Is Inaugurated Today." *St. Petersburg Times,* February 23, 2001, national section, p. A1.

Mills, R., English, A., and Fry, D. "USF Coach Is Accused of Bias." *St. Petersburg Times,* August 24, 2000, sports section C, p. 1.

JUDY GENSHAFT *has been president of the University of South Florida (Tampa) since July 2000.*

JACK WHEAT *served as special assistant to the president of the University of South Florida from 2000–2003.*

5

When a seemingly routine management decision sparks heated controversy on a college campus, the president must decide how to respond to students occupying a building and issuing an ultimatum to the administration.

Student Activism at Ithaca College: Reflections on Management and Leadership*

Peggy R. Williams, Michael R. McGreevey

Ithaca College (Ithaca, New York) is a private comprehensive residential college of about six thousand students located in the heart of the Finger Lakes region of upstate New York. Founded as a music conservatory in 1892, the college has retained its goal of providing a personal quality education for its students, even as it has grown in students and course offerings. The college actively strives to become the standard of excellence for residential comprehensive colleges, fostering intellect, creativity, and character in an active student-centered learning community (Ithaca College, 2000). The educational experience at Ithaca College is emphasized and realized both in and out of the classroom. Students are actively involved in research with faculty in many disciplines and engaged in internships and service learning related to course work. For their extracurricular life, they choose among a large number of clubs and athletic activities, including both varsity athletics and intramural sports.

In July 1997, I became president of Ithaca College, having previously served as the president of Lyndon State College in Lyndonville, Vermont. My background is somewhat unusual for a college president in that I started my professional career as a social worker. I have always valued community service, political activism, and civic-mindedness and was drawn to Ithaca College because of its commitment to community service and its full-time,

---

*Although much of this chapter is written in the first person, both authors contributed to the ideas and the writing.

traditional-age, residential student body, with all the energy and excitement that this population brings.

As part of my inauguration, we had a full day of community service activities the day before the inaugural ceremony in which students, faculty, and administrators participated in numerous activities both on and off campus. I wanted to develop a real sense of community, which by definition requires people to examine their own beliefs and attitudes, join in collegewide conversations, and participate in decision making. In my inaugural address, I talked about "knowing" as the capacity for learning and "knowing better" as the capacity for citizenship, here referring to the responsibility to the larger society. Throughout that year, when I met with student groups, I commended them for what they were doing and encouraged them to do more. Like their counterparts elsewhere, Ithaca students focused more attention on their academic studies or college life than on the larger issues of society or the world. Interest and active involvement in national and global issues had traditionally been at a low to moderate level on campus.

New Student Organizations Make Their Presence Felt

This changed abruptly in 2000. That spring, two new student groups were organized at Ithaca, the Young Democratic Socialists (YDS) chapter and "The Nine." The student arm of the Democratic Socialists of America, YDS was one of only about ten chapters on campuses across the country. The Ithaca YDS chapter was college-recognized; The Nine was an informal group of nine students, not a college-recognized student organization, but its membership overlapped and collaborated closely with YDS. Both organizations seemed to quickly evolve with little warning or indication. With their arrival, a new era in student activism began.

Although we were aware of YDS's presence on campus, we had not anticipated that this organization would find its major organizing event in a seemingly routine management decision that was being made that spring. In April 2000, the college entered into a multiyear contract with a new food service provider, Sodexho Marriott Services. Before selecting Sodexho Marriott, we had undertaken an extensive and competitive bidding process. We had engaged a third-party management consultant to cast the net widely to identify prospective providers and to evaluate their proposals and had assembled a committee of administrators and students to work together on the selection process, from putting together the request for proposal (RFP) to recommending the final choice of Sodexho Marriott to me. With the signing of the contract, college staff began to make arrangements for Sodexho Marriott to take over operations during the summer. Everything seemed to be moving along smoothly.

But not for long. Shortly after the announcement of Sodexho Marriott Services as Ithaca's new food service provider, students from the YDS organization began to raise questions regarding Sodexho Marriott's alleged ties to private prisons through its major stockholder, Sodexho Alliance, and their investments in Corrections Corporation of America (CCA). YDS students claimed that if we went with Sodexho Marriott Services, a certain percentage of every food service dollar spent at Ithaca College by a student would, in effect, go to the CCA to support the private prison industry. The students were strongly opposed to private prisons because they believed that there should never be a profit associated with incarceration. A profit motive, they argued, promoted an increase in incarcerations because they were good for the bottom line and discouraged spending on services, treatment, and staffing of prisons because they were not financially advantageous. To the students, privatizing prisons made them money-making ventures rather than rehabilitative or social services organizations.

The alleged connection of Sodexho Marriott Services to the private prison industry had never been raised during the RFP and decision-making process, so this accusation came to us entirely as a surprise. In fact, we soon learned that it was not known about elsewhere in higher education. We investigated the students' charges and learned that Ithaca's new food service provider, Sodexho Marriott Services, owned no stock in CCA. However, its parent company, Sodexho Alliances, did own 8 percent of CCA stock.

When the Ithaca board met in May, we told the trustees that we had chosen Sodexho Marriott Services as our new food service provider, explained the process we had used in selecting this company, and shared our excitement about the new food program opportunities that lay ahead. We also informed them of the students' concerns and explained to them what we had learned, that Sodexho Marriott did not own CCA stock. We thought the issue was now moot. On July 1, 2000, Sodexho Marriott took over the dining services, and the overall feedback from the campus community regarding the new food service provider was positive. Everyone praised the quality and selection of food and called the service excellent.

Student Activism Increases

But the students and the student protests returned in September. In the fall of 2000, energy from the YDS group increased. The students called for the college to sever its contract with Sodexho Marriott because of its alleged link with private prisons. We soon learned that they were supported in their efforts by two national groups, Democratic Socialists of America and the Prison Moratorium Project, an organization that lobbies state legislators against private prisons, as well as by some local labor unions. Throughout the fall, YDS attempted to persuade the student government association and other student clubs to join them in their crusade.

By the middle of the semester, the students' activities and intention were becoming increasingly public. Chalked messages appeared on sidewalks across campus; because they were a violation of the student conduct code, campus maintenance staff removed them as soon as they were discovered. Members of YDS and The Nine showed up at many campus events and disrupted campus admission tours, telling prospective students and their parents about the terrible practices of private prisons and claiming Ithaca College was supporting these abuses by using Sodexho Marriott. YDS passed out a petition across campus, and I began to receive numerous copies from students. Finally, after receiving about eighty of these form letters, I decided to set up a meeting. I invited all the students who had written me to join me in a classroom one afternoon to discuss their concerns. My goal was to educate myself about the issues on their minds and also to share with them what we had learned about the links between Sodexho Marriott Services and the investment decisions of Sodexho Alliance.

About forty to fifty students showed up for this meeting. From the students, I quickly learned, the issue was all about private prisons. They believed that their food service money supported CCA, and they objected strenuously to that. I tried to explain that the food service provider itself was not an investor in CCA, but they did not want to hear this information. The conversation was serious and civil, but I left feeling frustrated that the students seemed not to be interested in a closer examination of Sodexho Marriott's relationship with Sodexho Alliance or with CCA.

That meeting did not resolve the students' issues, nor did the many conversations between college administrators and students that followed. The vice president for student affairs and campus life and the executive assistant to the president continued to meet with students to keep an open dialogue. More than once in these conversations, students made reference to their intention to submit an ultimatum to the president, calling for Ithaca College to sever its contract with Sodexho Marriott Services, and they were advised that although they could do as they saw fit, this approach would not be constructive. On December 1, I received a letter of ultimatum calling for the immediate severance of the college's contract with Sodexho Marriott. YDS also announced a campus rally to be held on December 6 to gain support for the ultimatum.

After conferring with senior staff, we decided that it would be best for me not to be on campus on the day of the rally, so I made plans to work elsewhere that day. We did nothing to prevent the rally from taking place but made sure that campus security was on full alert in case of disturbances. The rally was well attended. Members of YDS spoke, along with one of the leaders of the Prison Moratorium Project. Shortly after the rally had ended, a group of students entered the administration building. The doors to the president's office on the third floor were locked; the doors to the Admissions Office, located on the first floor just inside the main entrance to the building, were open. Six Ithaca College students and one former student on leave that semester to work for the Democratic Socialists of America entered the Admissions Office and announced to the surprised admissions staff that "We're here, and we don't intend to leave until the president acts on our ultimatum." The admissions staff stayed in the office and told the students not to interfere with their business. As the day went on, news of the students' occupation of the office spread and gathered the support and curiosity of hundreds of members of the campus community, media, and others. Again, an ultimatum was presented to the vice president for student affairs and campus life and the executive assistant to the president.

Negotiating an Agreement

I remained off campus but was in ongoing phone contact with key senior administrators, including the vice president for student affairs and campus life, executive assistant to the president, director of public information, dean of enrollment planning, director of campus safety, and vice president and college counsel. Without a formally documented crisis-management plan, this group functioned as a team to monitor and respond to the immediate situation. Meanwhile, my office and home were flooded with hundreds of e-mails and phone calls, both local and national in origin, attacking Ithaca College for our support of private prisons. The mail attacked me for the terrible things they thought I was doing and told me what I should do if I had any morals at all. The letters skipped over Sodexho Marriott's connection to Sodexho Alliance and Sodexho Alliance's investment in CCA and saw Ithaca College as directly responsible for CCA's activities. The communications were remarkably alike in their wording and message. It was clear to me at this point that this was a well-organized national campaign with a clear agenda.

The central and ongoing question we faced as an administrative team was whether we would forcibly remove the students from the Admissions Office. As we came to the close of that first day, we decided not to do this. Although we would not treat the students who were occupying the Admissions Office like they were guests in a hotel, we did not want to use force to oust them. We continued to give them opportunities to leave, hoping they would choose to leave voluntarily, and they showed no signs of doing so.

The next day, with the students still occupying the Admissions Office, we cancelled some admissions appointments and moved other interviews to a different location. We seemed to be at a standstill. I was interested in having a conversation with the students, and the students refused to talk until I had signed the ultimatum. I repeatedly conveyed to them, through my administrative team, that I would never sign the ultimatum because signing an ultimatum is not the right way to make a decision. I wanted to sit down face to face with the students to talk. In the late afternoon, I received a call from the administrative team. Nothing was happening, they reported. I asked to talk directly to the students over the phone. When the students agreed, I got on the phone with them and explained that I would be glad to come talk with them in person. I kept explaining that if I agreed to their requirements and signed the ultimatum first, there would be nothing to talk about, and I would not make a decision under these circumstances. Finally, they agreed to meet.

In the early evening, I arrived under the escort of the director of public safety and was brought into the Admissions Office through a back door. The agreement I had made was that only I, the students, and the vice president for student affairs and campus life would meet, and no one else. In our conversation, I repeated over and over that we were not going to decide at that moment, as they wanted, to sever the contract with Sodexho Marriott Services. We talked for more than two hours. The vice president and I explained the considerable cost that would be involved in breaking a contract and starting all over to select a new food service provider, but the students did not care about the expense; this was a larger moral issue to them. Finally, we were able to reach agreement on a time frame for making the decision about whether to continue with Sodexho Marriott Services.

All my life I have been a note taker. It is the way I keep my attention on the topic under discussion and is a long-ingrained habit. This night was no different. As we debated differing points, I was the one person in the room writing them down. When we reached agreement on six action steps, I crafted the statement in front of the students. We reviewed it together and approved it as a group. We typed it up in the Admissions Office and then gave copies to ourselves and released it to the campus and the local press.

Thirty-four hours after the occupation had begun, the peaceful conclusion to the sit-in was brought about through these negotiations. Our six-point agreement read as follows:

The administration will conduct thorough research on the issue of private prisons and the relationship of Sodexho Marriott Services to private prisons.

There will be a well-advertised, college-sponsored forum in early to mid-February 2001 on the topics mentioned above.

The president will facilitate the most effective way to have the YDS position presented to the Ithaca College board of trustees by its February 2001 meeting.

President Williams will write a letter to Sodexho Alliance and share student concerns about these issues. A YDS representative will have the opportunity to review a draft of this letter.

The college will make its decision with regard to signing the YDS proposal on or before March 19.

The parties agree to establish check-in dates to ensure that progress is made on all these points.

In January we hired a communications and research specialist familiar with higher education and sent him out to research everything, from how the money flowed to CCA to what were the issues about private prisons.

During this period, we learned that students at a few other campuses that used Sodexho Marriott Services were following Ithaca's lead in raising the issue of the private prison industry. Arizona State University was one such institution; in the small world of higher education, its president, Lattie Coor, and I knew each other from when we were both presidents in Vermont. He had been president of the University of Vermont when I was at Lyndon State College. Because we were well ahead of Arizona State in investigating this controversy, I was glad to share what we learned with him. One thing we found out was that Sodexho Alliance was strongly considering divesting itself of CCA stock. They did not share their timetable for doing this, but we understood that this would likely be happening. The value of the stock had declined sharply in recent years, and it was no longer a lucrative holding.

The public forum specified in the negotiated agreement took place in February. A representative from the Prison Moratorium Project spoke, as did the legal counsel for Sodexho Marriott Services. An Ithaca College faculty member served as moderator; I attended but did not speak.

Reaching a Decision

When we had reviewed all the information that had been collected, it was clear to us that Sodexho Marriott Services was not an investor in private prisons. It seemed clear also that Ithaca College as an institution was not expert about the efficacy of private prisons and that we should not take an institutional position on this issue. In some ways, it was ironic that I would be the president to make this decision, given that my background is in social work and my husband is a criminal attorney. But I returned to the question of whether this was an issue on which the college should take a stand, and I felt that it was not.

On March 19, I announced that Ithaca College would retain the services of Sodexho Marriott Services as its dining services provider. Before the public announcement, I met in person with representatives of YDS to share my decision, and I provided them a copy of the press release of my announcement. I did not anticipate that they would be pleased with this outcome. They made no comments and asked no questions after I finished speaking. Then I sent the announcement via e-mail to the entire college community with an extensive statement attached that offered a thorough presentation of the information underlying this decision as well as other relevant information. This press release was also posted on a Web site.

The statement outlined our considerations in reaching the decision. With regard to private prisons, I wrote:

> The examination of the issues associated with private prisons has been an important learning opportunity for all involved: administrators, faculty, staff, and—we hope—students. We have learned that this is an important and

complex topic, and that simple nostrums do not apply . . . experts attest that the kinds of abuses of prisoners and other problems reported in private prisons occur in public prisons to a comparable degree. Such unacceptable treatment of human beings appears to be a moral issue for the corrections system in general.

More importantly, we have learned that the very existence of private prisons reflects a much larger social problem. Current federal and state criminal statutes and corrections policies—which to a great extent are supported and inspired by public opinion—are the driving forces behind the high rates of incarceration in this country and the ever-increasing demand for beds to house the growing prison population. In this environment, the private prison industry serves as a "quick release valve," providing . . . extra space that can be used to accommodate additional prisoners. Thus, the real support for private prisons is our tax dollars. . . . In my view, effectively addressing our concerns about rates of incarceration and the treatment of prisoners requires that we focus our energy and attention on those who make and implement public policy in this realm—primarily state and federal elected officials—and on activities that promote social justice. Focusing on the issue of private prisons only distracts us from these more important tasks and does not address the larger problem.

The statement also discussed other considerations, namely the quality of the food and services Sodexho Marriott Services was providing and the costs that would be incurred and disruption that would be experienced were the college to cancel the food service contract. Finally, I talked about the role of the college with regard to "social screening." Noting that colleges and universities were often pressured to become actors on behalf of various social causes, I explained that Ithaca College had "implemented forms of 'social screening' in cases where . . . investments or business activities can be seen to have a direct relationship with abuses of human rights." As one example, Ithaca College had endorsed the Sullivan Principles in the 1980s, divesting its stock holdings in companies doing business in South Africa that did not abide by these principles. After careful consideration of the Sodexho Marriott food service contract, we had determined that this case did "not rise to the standard of directness employed by the college in its decision to subscribe to the Sullivan Principles."

I concluded the statement by suggesting what I believed were appropriate ways for Ithaca College to "contribute to social justice." I instructed our newly hired full-time coordinator of community service and leadership development to evaluate our current community service activities and identify new programs in the area of social justice. I encouraged student organizations to sponsor programs on the criminal justice system and related social issues. I asked the provost to convene a group of faculty and deans to discuss "ways to incorporate our learning on these issues into the curriculum and opportunities through special courses, independent studies, or other mechanisms for students to pursue their interests in social justice and inequities of the criminal justice system," and called on the vice president for institutional advancement to help identify financial support for specific projects. In closing, I wrote:

> I hope that the Ithaca College community has learned, through this process, the importance of respectful and constructive dialogue. As an institution of higher learning, we are devoted to the advancement of knowledge and the search for truth. These can be achieved only if we remain open to new learning and are willing to listen seriously to divergent points of view. This is true especially when it comes to discussions of social issues, which always are complex and often are contested. Such discussions are enhanced by open, direct, and honest dialogue—the only kind that ultimately can lead to concerted and effective social action.

The general reaction from the campus community was positive regarding the thorough review of the situation and the comprehensive nature of the decision communiqué. In May an unrecognized referendum to again persuade the college administration to sever ties with Sodexho Marriott Services was held on campus. During the summer of 2000, the management of Sodexho Marriott notified the college that Sodexho Alliance had sold all its stock in CCA.

Reflections and Lessons Learned

As with any significant experience or change, it is valuable to take the opportunity to reflect, evaluate, and draw lessons from it for the future. As we reviewed this specific case, we identified a series of key points for consideration and future planning.

Development and Maintenance of an Emergency or Crisis-Management Plan. Although some areas of the college had developed a formal and documented plan for managing a crisis, it became apparent that such a plan for all key areas, as well as an overall plan for the institution, did not exist and should be developed. A team was selected and charged with the development of an emergency management plan.

Creation of a Core Emergency Response Team. As noted in the case, college personnel had responded successfully to this emergency. To maximize the best response to future critical situations, it was decided that a group would be established and function as the institution's Core Emergency Response Team. This group was charged with the development of the emergency or crisis-management plan and will oversee its implementation. In addition, we developed a list of key resources that could be called on for assistance or consultation.

Development of a Communications Plan. The exercise of internal and external communications was carried out on a case-by-case basis during this and other situations. We decided that it would best serve the college to have a well-documented communications plan for use during times of emergency, including dedication of a chief spokesperson(s), establishment of key messages, and a predetermined contact method or model.

Development of a Major Event Management Strategy. Working closely with the Office of Campus Safety and other appropriate areas, we established a plan to provide leadership, communications, and event management for major campus events or any event deemed controversial or with the "potential" for problems.

Assessment of the President's Role. Although this case is situational, it is important to have the president's role as clearly defined as possible. Certainly, the president is expected to provide leadership and direction, but what form should this take? Questions such as the following should be considered: When does the president speak to the press? When does the president enter into negotiations? Where is the president located during a crisis situation?

Working with Students. This group of students attempted to paint the administration as uncaring and unresponsive to the needs and interests of students. Although they were not able to attract the interest of most of the students to their cause, they attempted to create a coalition of other students and organizations to demonstrate solidarity and numbers. Strong and effective communication by the administration with student leaders, as well as appropriate accessibility and outreach to students and student leaders (Student Government Association meetings, and so forth) is essential on an ongoing basis. It is also important to pay attention or be "in tune" to small issues before they become big ones. Other areas for consideration include strategies for working together during times of disagreement or controversy, a clear understanding of the limits for acceptable student activism, the role of the student club advisor, and the like.

Student Activism: How Do We "Really" Feel About It? As mentioned earlier, it is part of the college's mission as an institution of higher learning to teach students to be involved, to question, to analyze, and to be an active part of the learning process. Along with this, it is important to teach and demonstrate the social norms and rules of civility and how to engage in a dialogue in which differences of opinion can be respected. The creative tension between "student" activism and the boundaries of responsible behavior within a community will always remain in a delicate balance.

Management by Ultimatum. This group of students was willing to communicate only by issuing an "only-one-answer-is-acceptable" ultimatum. This type of activism is clearly not acceptable or productive. It needs to be made clear that this is not the appropriate manner for doing business or communicating in the college environment or the larger society. By reinforcing the concept of communication and dialogue, these types of situations may be avoided.

Explore and Use Best Practices and Collegial Experience. During this period, it was especially helpful to work with colleagues on other campuses and learn from their specific or related experiences. In addition, it was mutually beneficial to maintain good communication with neighboring institutions of higher education.

Normalizing Relations. After a significant event such as the one described, it is important that operations and relations return to a normal and appropriate level as soon as possible. This demonstrates confidence and comfort to the community and the importance of systems and protocols. For example, students should be directed to the appropriate office or area for response or information. During this time of heightened student activism, the group of students called for and ultimately received a great amount of attention from members of the senior administration and president. If this is not reflective of the culture or the daily way of doing business, it is important to return to the "typical" way of communicating as soon as possible.

Review and Evaluation. This is one of the most important and valuable parts of any complex situation. At the conclusion of this situation, a thorough evaluation of the systems in place, resources available, and response took place. This reflective exercise proved valuable for the college's planning for the future. As a result of this specific incident, several lessons were learned, processes evaluated, and plans established for future implementation if necessary.

Final Analysis

Much has been said of the generation of students currently on our campuses. It has been our experience that our current students have high expectations of their relationship with the institution. Many view their relationship as a transactional one. Some have lost faith in leaders of our society. Although educators find this disturbing, it cannot be ignored and must be understood. Issues raised in this case—students' expectations, active participation, communication within a campus community, values, civility, leadership style—may be universal within the academy as a whole but must be examined and exercised within the context of the respective campus culture(s).

The situation recounted here was a difficult one. During the sit-in, the situation was all-consuming for those involved. Our commitment to civil dialogue, thorough analysis, and respect for process was critical to working through the issue at hand and remaining true to some personal beliefs as well as basic tenets of the academy.

Reference

Ithaca College. *Ithaca College Vision Statement*. Ithaca, N.Y.: Ithaca College, 2000.

PEGGY R. WILLIAMS has been president of Ithaca College, Ithaca, New York, since July 1997.

MICHAEL R. MCGREEVY has been the executive assistant to the president at Ithaca College since 1999.

6

The decision whether to keep or to change a university's nickname is an "intense no-win situation" for a new president. To some, the name is racist and insensitive; to others, it reflects great pride and tradition.

Miami Redskins: Deciding About a University Nickname

Paul G. Risser

PART I: CONFRONTING VALUE CONFLICTS

Miami University, chartered in 1809, opened its doors with twenty-four students in 1824. Its beautiful residential campus is located in Oxford in southwestern Ohio, in the valley of the Little Miami and Great Miami rivers. These rivers were named for the native Miami Indians, who lived in the region from 1700 until most of the tribe was forcefully removed to Kansas in 1840 and then to Oklahoma in 1867. It is from this region and for these people that Miami University is named. Today Miami is a selective, liberal education, doctoral university with twenty thousand students on three campuses.

On arriving as Miami's nineteenth president on January 1, 1993, almost immediately I encountered the continuing and frequently heated topic concerning the name of the university's athletic teams, the Miami Redskins. To many people, the term is considered racist or at least highly insensitive; to others, it is a name reflecting great pride in the region and in the native peoples for whom the university is named.

For most of Miami's first hundred years, the nickname was not an issue because the teams were referred to as simply Miami, Big Red, or similar names. In 1916, the athletic teams were described as the Big Red Team, but

---

The events described in part I of this chapter contributed to the chapter, "Confronting Value Conflicts," in J. B. McLaughlin (ed.), *Leadership Transitions: The New College President,* New Directions for Higher Education, no. 93, published by Jossey-Bass Publishers, 1996.

the college yearbook, *Recensio,* was designed with an Indian motif, and key seniors were identified as "Big Chiefs." The yearbook contained the "Scalp Song," coauthored by Alfred Upham, who later became the fourteenth president of the university. In the intervening years, there were no Indian motifs in the yearbook until the 1923 version, when pictures of Indian sculptures appeared. In 1927, the term "Tribe Miami" was first used, there were pictures of students dressed as Indians, and the athletic lettermen were described as Tribe Miami.

In 1931, the term "Redskin" appeared in the *Recensio.* In 1932, the Redskin logo appeared, first on cheerleaders' uniforms and then on various campus images. The 1936 *Alumni News* states that "Miami reveled in the name 'Big Reds' until 1928 when R. J. McGuiness, Miami publicity director, coined the term 'Redskins.' " Thus, the term Redskin has an informal origin, and it began when the university was about 120 years old.

From about 1930 until the early 1970s, the use of the term Redskin and several related symbols spread in many directions, including a mascot called "Hia-wa-bop," a costumed warrior, from the 1950s to 1972. In 1972, the university's seventeenth president, Phillip R. Shriver, appointed a task force to examine the use of the name Redskin and associated issues. As a result of these deliberations, use of the term Redskin was reaffirmed, although Hia-wa-bop was abolished as the mascot, to be replaced by Chief Miami; this individual was to be trained in dance by the Miami Tribe and to be costumed in authentic fancy dancer regalia. The university also adopted a policy eliminating all derogatory caricatures of Indians and stated that "all dress and activities depicting Indians at athletic events or wherever Indian symbols are used must be authentic, dignified, and in good taste."

Miami University has a unique and close relationship with the federally recognized Miami Tribe of Oklahoma, from which it received its name. This relationship is an unusually sincere and personal one. The university takes great pride in the tribe, and current and past students speak in caring ways about the tribe. The tribe considers Miami to be "their university," the chief and other members of the tribe frequently visit the university, and a few young people from the tribe attend Miami. The university and the tribe mutually treasure and respect this strong relationship and continually seek to enhance their partnership.

Background: Early Spring 1993

Early in the spring semester of 1993, shortly after my arrival, the university senate passed a resolution stating that the term Redskin would no longer be used as the nickname of the university's athletic teams. Under university procedures, such resolutions are forwarded to the board of trustees through the president, who may choose to offer a recommendation. At about this time, the student newspaper, *The Miami Student,* decided and stated that it would no longer use the term Redskin in its publication.

Several circumstances triggered these events. Mascot names were being debated at several colleges, and there was ongoing national discussion about the Washington Redskins, the Atlanta Braves, and the Cleveland Indians. At Miami, a number of student leaders, including the president of the Associated Student Government, took up the challenge of forcing the university to abandon the name Miami Redskins. In addition, because I was a new president who arrived from New Mexico and was a native of Oklahoma, many felt that, from this close association with Native Americans, I would be more receptive to a change in the name of the mascot.

Deciding Whether or Not to Engage the Issue. At this point, I considered several options as president. In brief, the options were to transmit the senate's resolution to the board without any recommendations, make a unilateral decision either to retain or eliminate the nickname, engage in thorough discussion before making a decision, or ignore the issue in any formal manner and let the various points of view be argued in spontaneous forums.

The simplest decision would have been to pass along the senate's resolution to the board of trustees without any recommendation. Although the outcome is uncertain, after heated discussion at one or more board meetings, the board would likely have voted to retain the name. Adopting this option would have shielded the president from much of the pressure: the constituent groups would have aimed their most intensive lobbying and arguments at the board, whose members would have made the final decision.

If the president had made a unilateral decision to retain the Redskin name, the board would likely have upheld the decision; if the president had decided to change the name, the board would probably not have upheld the decision. In either case, the losing side would have argued vehemently that its position was not heard and that it was treated unfairly. Moreover, the losing side would probably not have changed its practices. That is, if the decision had been to eliminate the term Redskin from use, it would have continued to appear clandestinely, as has happened at other institutions when unilateral decisions have been made. A more interesting political option, of course, would have been for the president to have decided to eliminate the name Redskin and then to have the board overturn this decision. In this instance, the president would have satisfied those who wanted to eliminate the term, and the board would have satisfied those who wished to retain it.

As president, I could have (at least) attempted to ignore or delay the issue and not have brought forth the senate's recommendation. After making the legitimate argument that its wishes were being stonewalled, the senate would have requested an audience with the board, and it is likely that spontaneous demonstrations of various types would have arisen. If the senate had not raised the issue, it would have been raised by other constituencies on campus, and the options would have been the same, with proposals being presented directly to the board of trustees.

All three of these options would have left the board in the position of making a decision without the strong leadership of the president.

From the outset, it was abundantly clear that this was an intense no-win situation. There were strong and deep feelings on both sides, and both sides could not be simultaneously satisfied. In many ways, however, this issue is no different from others facing our society, such as abortion, gun control, welfare entitlement programs, or even foreign aid. Reasonable people, with strong moral and ethical values, come to very different decisions.

After considering the alternatives and asking myself if there were ways in which the situation could become part of an enriched learning experience, I concluded that the university should engage the issue. In so doing, Miami University had an opportunity to make a significant contribution to the resolution of issues such as these.

To be successful in developing a model for these complicated discussions and decisions, our process needed to provide an environment that encouraged open sharing of ideas and a respect for different points of view. Simply voting on the issue was not the point because this would not have involved additional learning. There should be an abundance of informed discussion in which the participants take the time and make the effort to study the issue, not simply leap to an initial position and defend that position at all costs.

Decision Process. Miami University used a thorough process for considering the use of the term Redskin that involved many constituencies and venues. A detailed package of information was placed on reserve in all the libraries, many discussion groups and sessions were organized, and the topic was discussed in several classes and in both student and commercial newspapers. Alumni chapters were sent information and urged to discuss the topic, as was the athletic booster club. The most widely advertised and attended event was a forum held in the field house in which about 120 speakers spoke for up to three minutes each. As president, I moderated the entire forum, recognizing each speaker, making notes as appropriate, and expressing appreciation for every statement. The forum was orderly, with different groups expressing support for statements with which they agreed and little or no disparagement of opposing views. All those who requested the opportunity to speak did so and, perhaps by chance, were evenly split between those who spoke for changing and those who spoke for retaining the name. A special session was held for the board of trustees in which its members heard presentations on both sides of the issue from representative students, staff, faculty, and alumni. In addition, persons were encouraged to write to the president and offer opinions and advice.

After all this consideration, there were those who sincerely believed that the name should be changed and those who thought it should be retained. Those who believed it should be changed argued one or more of the following points: the name is derogatory, racist, and insensitive; it conveys the wrong image of Native Americans; nicknames of athletic teams can be changed without harming the long-term identity of the institution; and a university, as a place where all people and ideas should be respected, should have no nicknames that denote otherwise. Those who believed in maintaining the status quo argued that the name was initially selected to honor the American Indians, that it is not meant to be negative and but connotes positive characteristics, that it has developed a strong and respectful tradition, that the use of the term does not mean disrespect and therefore the term cannot be disrespectful, and that the move to change it comes largely from a few people who are concerned about what is currently termed a "politically correct" point of view.

Several other universities and colleges also have considered changes in nicknames or symbols that denote Native Americans. In some cases, there has been change, and in others the status quo has been maintained. In virtually every one of these cases, regardless of the ultimate decision, the issue has remained divisive, in some cases for years and even decades. This is not surprising, especially when decisions have been made without inclusive and comprehensive consideration. Conflict over the issue continues because there is no answer that satisfies all parties, nor is there an objective method for deciding what all persons should think or believe.

Role of the Miami Tribe. As recently as 1990, the Miami Tribe was asked for its opinion on the name Redskin, and it stated that it was agreeable to the continued use of the term. This was an important statement because many of those in this discussion argued that it should be left to the tribe to decide. That is, if the tribe had no disagreement with the continued use of the term, then it should be continued. In this more recent discussion in 1993, the tribe chose not to participate directly. As one would expect among any group of people, there were members of the tribe who believed the name should be changed, others thought it should be retained, and many had no particular opinion or believed the issue to be unimportant. The tribe, however, supported the process by which the issue was being considered and said it would support the decision made by the president.

Early in the process, the tribe indicated that if a change in the nickname were made, the tribe would ask that the symbolism between the university and the tribe persist and that any other nickname continue to convey the strong relationship between the university and the tribe. If no change were made in the name, the tribe would ask that the name Redskin continue to be used with the utmost care and respect.

Institutional Values and the Decision

The nickname is not the fundamental issue in itself; it is a manifestation of personal beliefs and of institutional values. There is a serious question about the degree to which an institution should attempt to dictate the beliefs and statements of its members and constituents. An academic institution by its nature is committed to free inquiry and to promoting a search for knowledge. While recognizing the dignity of individual members of the community, an academic institution is not and should not be engaged in promoting a particular ideology or denying individuals the right to hold unpopular positions. Fundamental to the process of learning is the ability of an individual to question the conventional wisdom, to refine the teachings being offered, and to derive his or her own values.

At Miami University, it is our fundamental position that individuals should become as informed as possible on issues in question, should recognize their individual responsibility to society as a whole as well as to themselves, and should develop a set of values on which to make judgments and base decisions. The role of the university is to provide an environment that supports this personal intellectual development, including the ability to make decisions and to anticipate and accept the consequences of those decisions.

Decision. Miami University retains as one of its hallmarks an intellectual environment that encourages respectful and informed debate. Indeed, a major purpose of this university is to assist students as they clarify their values and reach responsible decisions. In this environment, all the participants, be they students, faculty staff, parents, alumni, or community members, are expected as individuals to form views and beliefs based on thoughtful analysis and sound moral judgments. Thus, in my opinion, each person should be called on to decide whether he or she wishes to use the term Redskin. This individual decision should be based on careful and informed thought, the values of the person, *and* his or her responsibilities to others and to society.

Miami University also has values and responsibilities. One of its responsibilities is to value its people and to ensure that these persons can grow intellectually in a reasoned, fair, and respectful environment. Appellations help create this environment. To many, the nickname Redskin implies a disrespectful environment. Conversely, to others the nickname does not imply any disrespect. Therefore, as an institution that encourages independent thought, as president, I decided that the institutional use of the term Redskin as a nickname for the university's athletic teams would be addressed in the following way:

> First, only university athletic organizations and athletic publications currently using the nickname Redskin may continue to use the nickname. Whenever the term Redskin is used, the name and any symbol of peoples and cultures must continue to be represented authentically, with dignity and respect. The use of the nickname Redskin shall not be expanded beyond representations where it currently appears.
>
> Second, all other organizations sponsored by the university and official publications of the university not covered above will use the term Miami Tribe as the nickname of the athletic teams. The word *tribe* is defined by Webster's in part as "A group of persons, families, or clans believed to be descended from a common ancestor and forming a close community." This clearly describes the unique relationship between Miami University and the

Miami Tribe of Oklahoma, and it responds to the tribe's request that the name retain the symbolism between the tribe and the university. The nickname Miami Tribe provides an alternative for those who believe that the term Redskin does not convey the sensitive environment that must exist at Miami University. The university's linkage with a proud Native American people, even in the name of the institution, can be preserved with dignity indefinitely through the use of the words Miami Tribe.

Discussion. It would have been relatively easy for me to have made a simple decision either to discard or retain the Redskin name, but neither of these outcomes, although they would have engendered approval from some quarters, would have been the right decision. Had that happened, one part of the community would have won and another part would have lost. There would have been continued discussion because the university would have attempted to dictate beliefs to individuals, to state what is right or wrong, when in fact the answer must come from individual values and judgments. Far more significantly, each of us would suddenly have been absolved of thinking about the implications of this issue any further. By providing an alternative, the university does not divide the community. More important, as a result of this recommendation, each of us as a person, as members of campus athletic organizations, or through involvement with athletic publications was required to continue to examine our values and responsibilities, decide how we use words, and reflect on how our thoughts and ideas affect and are affected by other people and cultures.

The process of considering this issue was extremely important as a model for discussing complex topics, and the university involved its broad community in resolving it. Acceptance of the nickname Redskin has been reasserted when individuals, athletic organizations, and those involved with athletic publications have carefully considered the implications as brought forth during the deliberative process. Alternatively, the term Tribe may be used by those who prefer it; its use is also supported by the Miami Tribe of Oklahoma. As part of the recommendation, I established a task force to make recommendations to strengthen the relationship between the tribe and the university. Most of the task force recommendations have now been implemented.

Action of the Board of Trustees. After considerable discussion at the designated meeting, the board of trustees voted to accept the president's recommendation. The vote was four positive, three negative, one abstention, and one absentee positive vote that was not officially counted. This close vote reflected the continued division of opinion on the issue, even after exhaustive and extended discussion.

My recommendation was a surprise to virtually all in the community; it had been widely expected that the answer would be to either continue or discontinue the name. The initial reaction was either that the decision was no decision at all or that it was a reasonable compromise. Over time, others have come forth to applaud the recommendation, and if a poll were taken today, there would be a significant number of people in all of these camps.

During the past year and a half, the issue of the nickname has arisen only occasionally on campus and throughout the broader community. The term Tribe is rarely used, and Redskin or simply Miami is the predominant term used for the university's athletic teams.

Concluding Thoughts

Discussion of the Redskin issue consumed a large amount of time and energy. Thus, a reasonable question is whether it was worth all the effort and, if we were to do it again, whether the issue should have been raised. Of course, there is no experimental control; that is, one cannot predict the situation today had we not decided to engage the issue.

On the negative side, much time and energy were devoted to this issue, and thus, there may have been opportunity costs in terms of what could have been accomplished otherwise. Questions were raised as to whether the new president understood the tradition of the Redskins and whether such an issue should be raised so early in his term or even if the issue should ever be raised. And there was some polarization on the campus, although without exception, this resulted in civilized exchanges. Many of those most strongly interested in encouraging diversity on campus were disappointed that the name was not changed, thereby sending a strong message that diversity was welcomed and encouraged. It should be noted, however, that there were ethnic minorities on both sides of the issue.

On the positive side, the campus and the community were able to discuss a volatile issue in great depth and with strong passion but to do so in a civilized manner. In addition, this process led by the president signaled that the campus would be open to serious debate but that such discussion should be based on information and judgments rather than on emotion and previously held views. There are no quantitative data, but it appeared that a small number of participants changed their opinions, especially in the direction of deciding that the term Redskin might not be appropriate at this time although it might have been acceptable at other times. Virtually everyone completed the process with a better understanding of the opposing opinion. The final decision permitted (indeed, forced) individuals to reexamine their own values and to think hard about their interactions with other peoples and cultures. Those who continued to believe the term Redskin was acceptable could continue to use it, and those who thought it unacceptable had an alternative that met the expectations of the Miami Tribe.

So, on balance, if I were able to make the decision again, would we engage the issue? The answer is yes, but with even greater reluctance. Yes, because it is so important for universities, especially good ones, to provide opportunities for their members to engage in complicated issues and in so doing to learn from each other. This issue, and all its implications, is as important as any other for our students and for society at large. My reluctance arises from the great opportunity cost; that is, other important issues were neglected just because the Redskin issue required a disproportionate amount of time. Also, this issue was so dominant that it has taken much longer for me to set forth my own agenda for the university. However, had we not engaged the issue, we would still be dealing with it in smaller components, but it is unlikely that the total amount of time would have been as extensive.

PART II: THE DECISION IN RETROSPECT

As described above, in 1993 shortly after I became president of Miami University, the faculty senate passed a resolution declaring that the term "Redskin" would no longer be used as the nickname of the University's athletic teams. I decided that rather than make an immediate decision, the university would benefit from intellectually engaging the issue. This resulted in an enormous amount of discussion and much communication on campus and also among alumni groups, the public, and with and among the members of the board of trustees.

During this process, the Miami Tribe formally stated that it would accept the decision of the university (technically, the board of trustees). If the name were changed, the tribe wanted to keep the symbolism between the university and the tribe. If the Redskin name was not changed, the tribe requested that the name be used with the utmost care and respect.

The Decision in Late 1993. In virtually every venue and discussion, the views were essentially equal between those who wanted to change the name and those who did not. Although a vote was never taken on just this issue among the trustees, it is highly unlikely that the board would have voted to change the name. In the end, I decided that the name of the Miami Redskins could remain in its current usage with athletic teams and publications, as long as it was used with respect. All other university-sponsored publications and organizations could adopt the term "Miami Tribe" as a symbol of the university's long-standing connection with the tribe. The Miami Tribe supported the decision and indicated its pleasure with the use of Miami Tribe. In December, the board of trustees accepted my recommendation in a split vote that indicated its support of the recommendation but also revealed the continued reluctance of some members to diminish the use of the Miami Redskins name.

Actions Taken in 1996 and 1997. I left Miami University for the presidency of Oregon State University, Corvallis, beginning January 1, 1996. Six months later, in July 1996, the Miami Tribe passed a resolution saying it could no longer support the use of Redskins as an athletic name. In September 1996, the Miami University board of trustees, citing its respect for the tribe, voted to discontinue the use of Redskins as a team nickname. The board requested that the new president, James Garland, recommend a new name. A committee was established to recommend the new name, and about seven hundred nicknames were suggested. After some contention, in April 1997 the trustees voted to adopt the "RedHawks" as the new name for the Miami athletic teams. The image of the Miami Indian head was retained and now appears on the football stadium and in other locations, sometimes with the new RedHawk symbol.

After the decision to eliminate the Redskin name, there were some continuing complaints, and a frivolous lawsuit was filed (and subsequently dropped). Today, the topic arises occasionally among alumni and athletics fans, but Miami University has moved on from the controversy.

1993 Decision Revisited. Looking back, would I go about the process in the same way and make the same decision? No.

Much has changed in the intervening years. More than half the high schools with racially explicit or racially connected mascot names have changed their name. On the other hand, many high schools and other institutions have not changed their mascot names. The range of names regarded as offensive has now expanded far beyond those related to American Indians and African Americans. A legislator in California recently introduced a bill that would prohibit the use of such names among high schools throughout the state. So although the environment has changed, the issue is still contentious.

In 1993, from an institutional point of view, it was not at all clear to me that the name of the Miami Redskins should necessarily be changed. I thoroughly understood the arguments on both sides and would have changed the name as a purely personal choice. But the pride taken in the name by the Miami Tribe seemed particularly important. In addition, I was uncomfortable that a university, a place where the community needs to learn by engaging issues and arriving at personal values, would simply dictate an answer—what people should think.

In retrospect, my approach was too idealistic. I put far too much faith in the presumed power of logic and informed discourse, and my notion of the educational value of debate was exaggerated. The idea that somehow a group of diverse people would ever arrive at a consensus on such an emotionally charged issue is simply unrealistic. The two sides in the debate would never come to agreement by mutual consent, and there were outspoken honorable people of strong moral character on both sides. Complicated issues such as this will persist indefinitely unless they are dealt with clearly and unambiguously.

Today I would actively manage the situation to come to a much more expeditious decision that put the university's simple institutional interests first. The institutional opportunity costs, both in negative publicity and distractions from other important endeavors, were simply too high. Moreover, the long-term consequences from the protracted discord among advocates for the university should always be minimized.

The two deciding participants in the decision were the Miami Tribe and the board of trustees. My first step would have been to determine if the Miami Tribe would express a more preferential view on one side of the argument (this is what eventually happened). Second, instead of trying to provide an answer for the board of trustees, I would work with them individually to arrive at a constructive consensus. The open process I chose looked constructive, but it actually subjected the trustees to considerable pressure as individuals. Third, I would have focused on making a decision more quickly instead of touting the theoretical advantages of extended public debate.

Perhaps this more managerial approach comes with the experience of serving two additional years as president of Miami University and another seven years as president of Oregon State University. In some ways, this change is unfortunate: my idealistic hope that people would learn more and confront their own value systems more powerfully from open debate still seems right on moral and ethical grounds. But today the major public universities are subjected to a whole host of political, economic, and ideological forces. The days of making major policy decisions in splendid isolation among ivy-covered walls surrounding contemplative intellectuals are gone at public universities. As presidents, our responsibilities have unfortunately turned from a focus on intellectual engagement and debate to ensuring the academic and financial integrity of the university. Leadership of large public universities today involves more and more management. Whereas we recognize this essential managerial dimension of leadership, I cling to the hope that as presidents, we occasionally will be allowed the luxury of allowing and even encouraging vigorous and messy debate about significant issues.

PAUL G. RISSER is chancellor of the Oklahoma State System of Higher Education.

INDEX

85

Back Issue/Subscription Order Form

Copy or detach and send to:

Jossey-Bass, A Wiley Company, 989 Market Street, San Francisco CA 94103-1741

Call or fax toll-free: Phone 888-378-2537 6:30AM – 3PM PST; Fax 888-481-2665

Back Issues: Please send me the following issues at $29 each

(Important: please include series initials and issue number, such as HE114.)

_____

_____

_____

$ _____   Total for single issues

$ _____   SHIPPING CHARGES: SURFACE   Domestic   Canadian

		Domestic	Canadian
	First Item	$5.00	$6.00
	Each Add'l Item	$3.00	$1.50

For next-day and second-day delivery rates, call the number listed above.

Subscriptions: Please __start __renew my subscription to *New Directions for Higher Education* for the year 2____at the following rate:

U.S.	__Individual $80	__Institutional $170
Canada	__Individual $80	__Institutional $210
All Others	__Individual $104	__Institutional $244

**For more information about online subscriptions visit
www.interscience.wiley.com**

$ _____   Total single issues and subscriptions (Add appropriate sales tax for your state for single issue orders. No sales tax for U.S. subscriptions. Canadian residents, add GST for subscriptions and single issues.)

__Payment enclosed (U.S. check or money order only)

__VISA __MC __AmEx #_____ Exp. Date _____

Signature _____ Day Phone _____

__ Bill Me (U.S. institutional orders only. Purchase order required.)

Purchase order # _____

Federal Tax ID13559302   GST 89102 8052

Name _____

Address _____

_____

Phone _____ E-mail _____

For more information about Jossey-Bass, visit our Web site at **www.josseybass.com**

**NEW DIRECTIONS FOR HIGHER EDUCATION
IS NOW AVAILABLE ONLINE AT WILEY INTERSCIENCE**

What is Wiley InterScience?

Wiley InterScience is the dynamic online content service from John Wiley & Sons delivering the full text of over 300 leading scientific, technical, medical, and professional journals, plus major reference works, the acclaimed *Current Protocols* laboratory manuals, and even the full text of select Wiley print books online.

What are some special features of Wiley InterScience?

Wiley InterScience Alerts is a service that delivers table of contents via e-mail for any journal available on Wiley InterScience as soon as a new issue is published online.
Early View is Wiley's exclusive service presenting individual articles online as soon as they are ready, even before the release of the compiled print issue. These articles are complete, peer-reviewed, and citable.
CrossRef is the innovative multi-publisher reference linking system enabling readers to move seamlessly from a reference in a journal article to the cited publication, typically located on a different server and published by a different publisher.

How can I access Wiley InterScience?

Visit http://www.interscience.wiley.com

Guest Users can browse Wiley InterScience for unrestricted access to journal Tables of Contents and Article Abstracts, or use the powerful search engine.
Registered Users are provided with a *Personal Home Page* to store and manage customized alerts, searches, and links to favorite journals and articles. Additionally, Registered Users can view free Online Sample Issues and preview selected material from major reference works.
Licensed Customers are entitled to access full-text journal articles in PDF, with select journals also offering full-text HTML.

How do I become an Authorized User?

Authorized Users are individuals authorized by a paying Customer to have access to the journals in Wiley InterScience. For example, a university that subscribes to Wiley journals is considered to be the Customer. Faculty, staff and students authorized by the university to have access to those journals in Wiley InterScience are Authorized Users. Users should contact their Library for information on which Wiley journals they have access to in Wiley InterScience.

ASK YOUR INSTITUTION ABOUT WILEY INTERSCIENCE TODAY!